AF248731

CHARLES M. RUSSELL

Masterpieces from the Amon Carter Museum

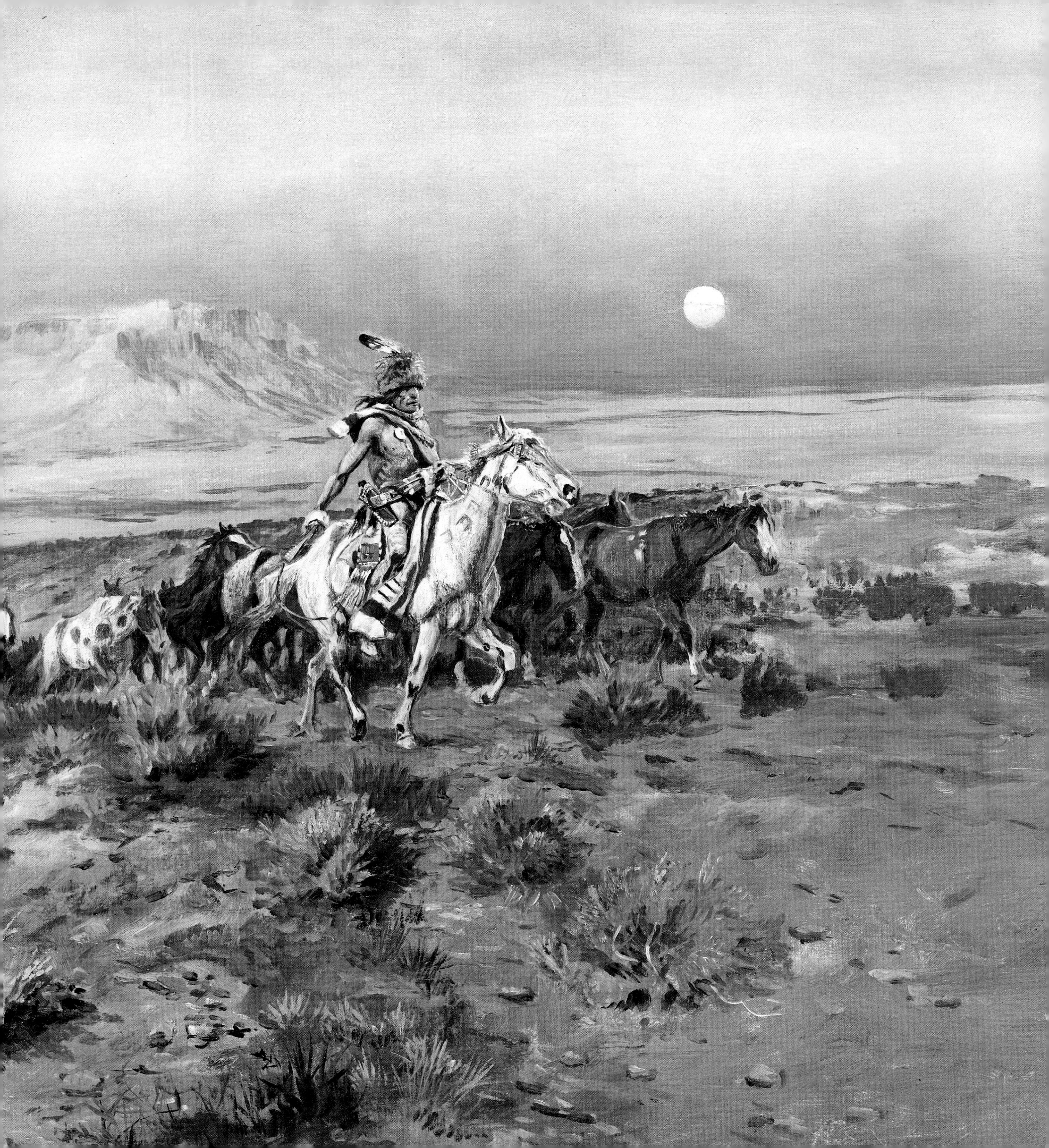

CHARLES M. RUSSELL

Masterpieces from the Amon Carter Museum

RICK STEWART

Curator of Western Painting and Sculpture, Amon Carter Museum

AMON CARTER MUSEUM

Fort Worth

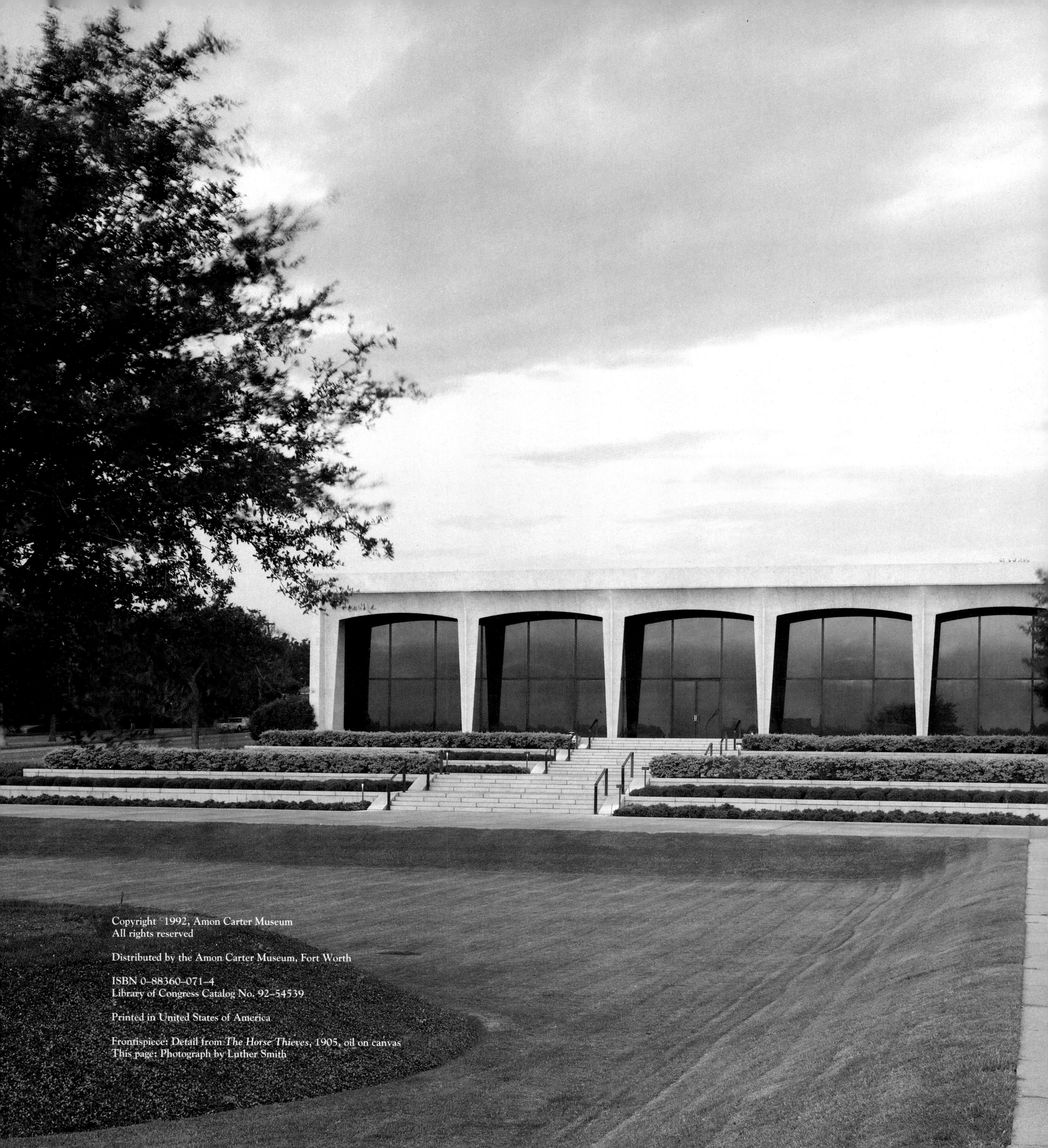

Distributed by the Amon Carter Museum, Fort Worth

ISBN 0–88360–071–4
Library of Congress Catalog No. 92–54539

Printed in United States of America

Frontispiece: Detail from *The Horse Thieves*, 1905, oil on canvas
This page: Photograph by Luther Smith

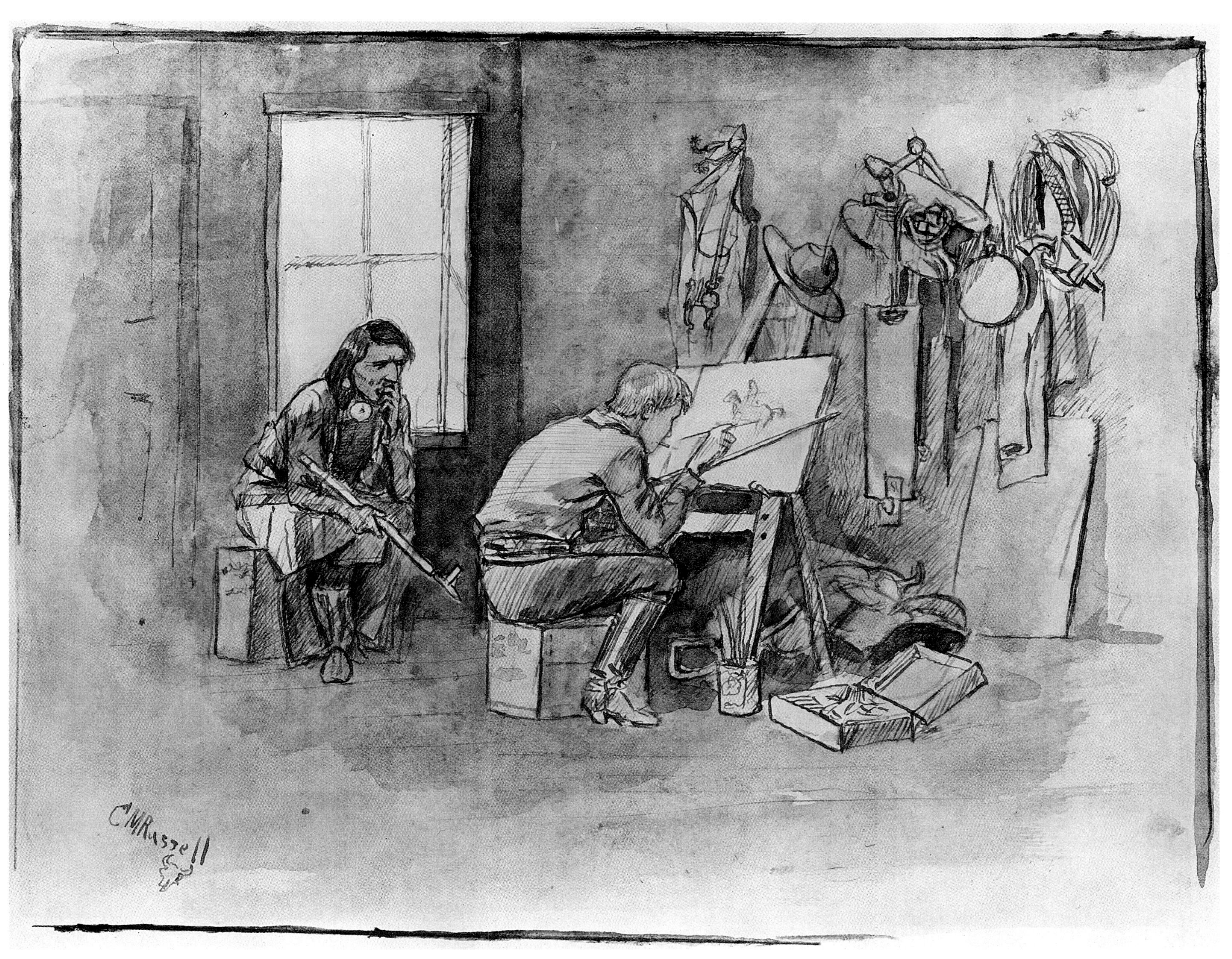

Contrast in Artist's Salons—Charlie Painting in His Cabin, c. 1894, ink wash and graphite

Will Rogers once related a story about the first time a Charles M. Russell painting brought a big price in the art market back East. Naturally the story circulated in the local newspapers, and one cowpuncher read the news and decided to call on the artist. "Charlie," he asked, "what is it that makes them pictures cost so much? Is it the brush or the paint?" According to Rogers, this was the kind of story Russell loved to repeat. Rogers, who could spin a pretty good yarn himself, thought his Montana friend the greatest storyteller he had ever heard. Indeed, Russell left a rich legacy in his stories and illustrated letters, one very much in the tradition of two earlier writers he admired, Bret Harte and Mark Twain.

At the same time, he managed to carry his narrative abilities over to his art. More than any western artist, save perhaps Frederic Remington, Russell defined many of the themes that constitute the larger view of the American West in the popular consciousness. The Indian, the cowboy, the frontier, the wilderness—all were essayed from a mixture of reality and fancy to become myth. At the same time, no artist ever conveyed a deeper level of romance in his work. Russell's vibrant paintings, with their lone figures silhouetted against a broad, dramatic landscape, exude the romance of the West. In this respect, his art deeply influenced the development of the western film. John Ford, the greatest director of film westerns, once observed that his movies transformed fact into legend. It is certainly true that Russell's paintings and stories were a precedent for that entire process. Will Rogers understood the importance of his friend's achievement. "He was the greatest artist the West has ever produced," Rogers wrote shortly after the artist's death. "He didn't go there to study the West, just to paint it. He loved it, lived it, and painted it because he loved it."

Will Rogers and Amon G. Carter, Sr., were close friends for many years, and it was Rogers who first introduced the Fort Worth publisher to the work of Charles M. Russell. In 1935, the year that Rogers lost his life in a tragic airplane accident, Carter acquired his first Russells—nine watercolors that had belonged to Harry E. Hayward, a boyhood friend of the artist, and Hayward's brother-in-law, George W. Niedringhaus, who owned a ranch in

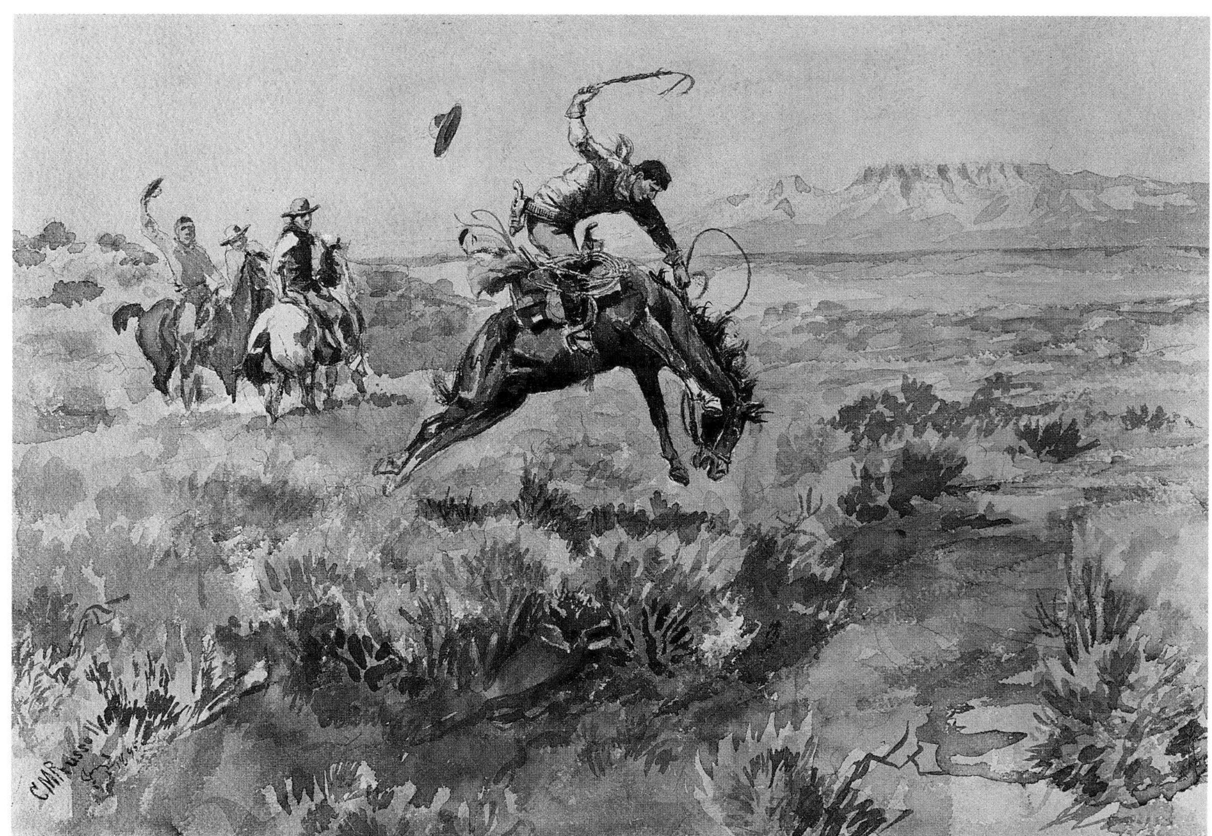

Bronco Busting, 1895, watercolor and graphite

The Picture Robe, 1899, pen and ink, and graphite on paper

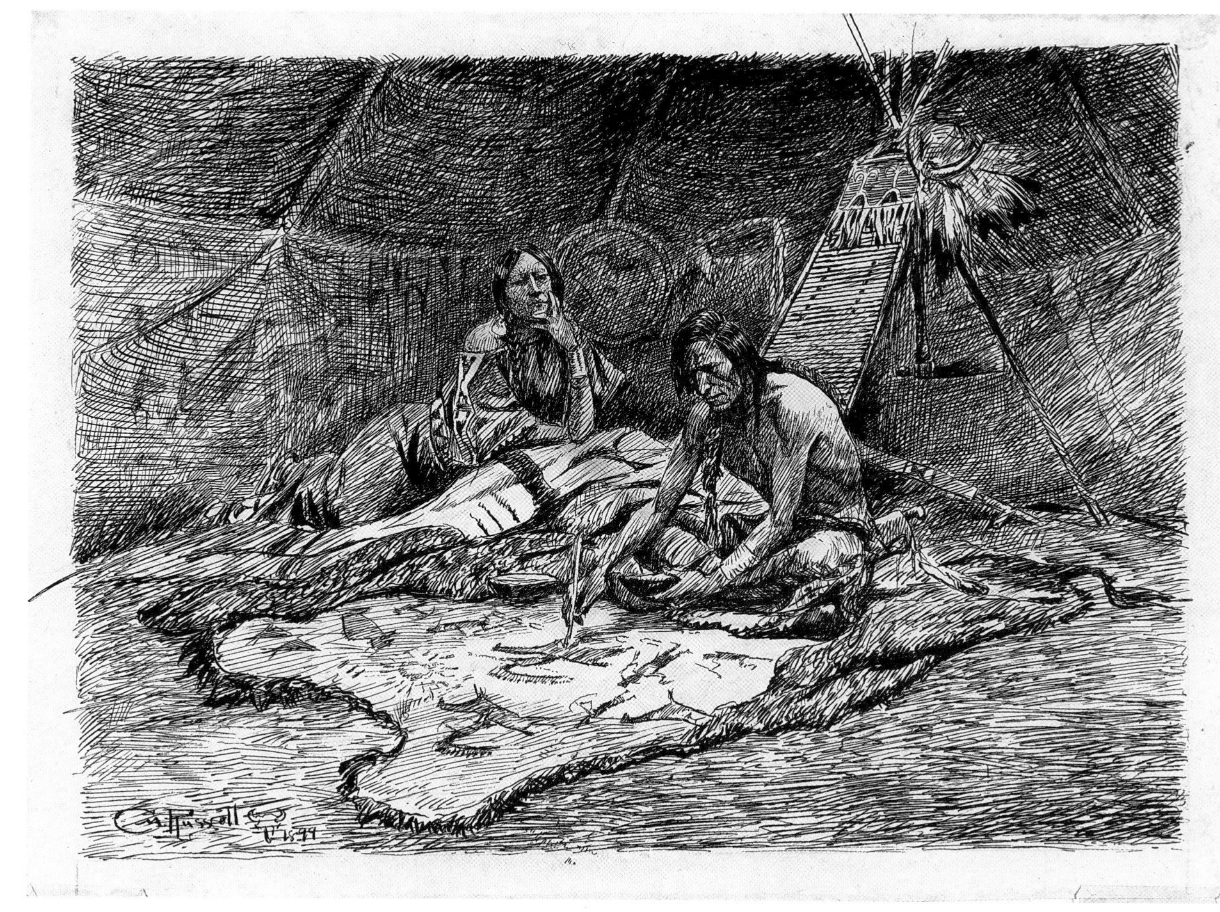

Montana where Russell had often worked. Within two years, Carter purchased seven additional paintings, watercolors, and drawings from the descendants of John A. Sleicher, the editor of *Leslie's Weekly*, who had commissioned the works from Russell in the early years of this century. From then on, Carter's interest in Russell quickened. Following the death of Nancy C. Russell at her home in Pasadena, California, in 1940, he acquired several objects from the estate, including one of the finest paintings that had hung in the house. C. R. Smith, an aviation industry pioneer and a close friend of Carter's, also purchased a large portion of the Russell estate, and in 1946 he sold Carter an important collection of sculpture—virtually the only complete set of the artist's bronzes then known—which had belonged to Nancy Russell.

On November 4, 1947, General Dwight D. Eisenhower unveiled a life-size bronze equestrian statue of Will Rogers, the gift of Amon Carter, on the Texas Centennial grounds west of downtown Fort Worth. Carter also acquired two magnificent Russell paintings that had belonged to Rogers, which he installed with the others on the walls of the Fort Worth Club. The collection of bronzes was put on display at the Fort Worth Public Library. Having decided several years before to establish a public museum for his growing western art collection, Carter continued to add to his Russell holdings. In 1952, he completed negotiations to obtain the famed collection of more than eighty of Russell's works that had belonged to Sid Willis, proprietor of the Mint Saloon in Great Falls, Montana. With this acquisition, Carter possessed the most significant

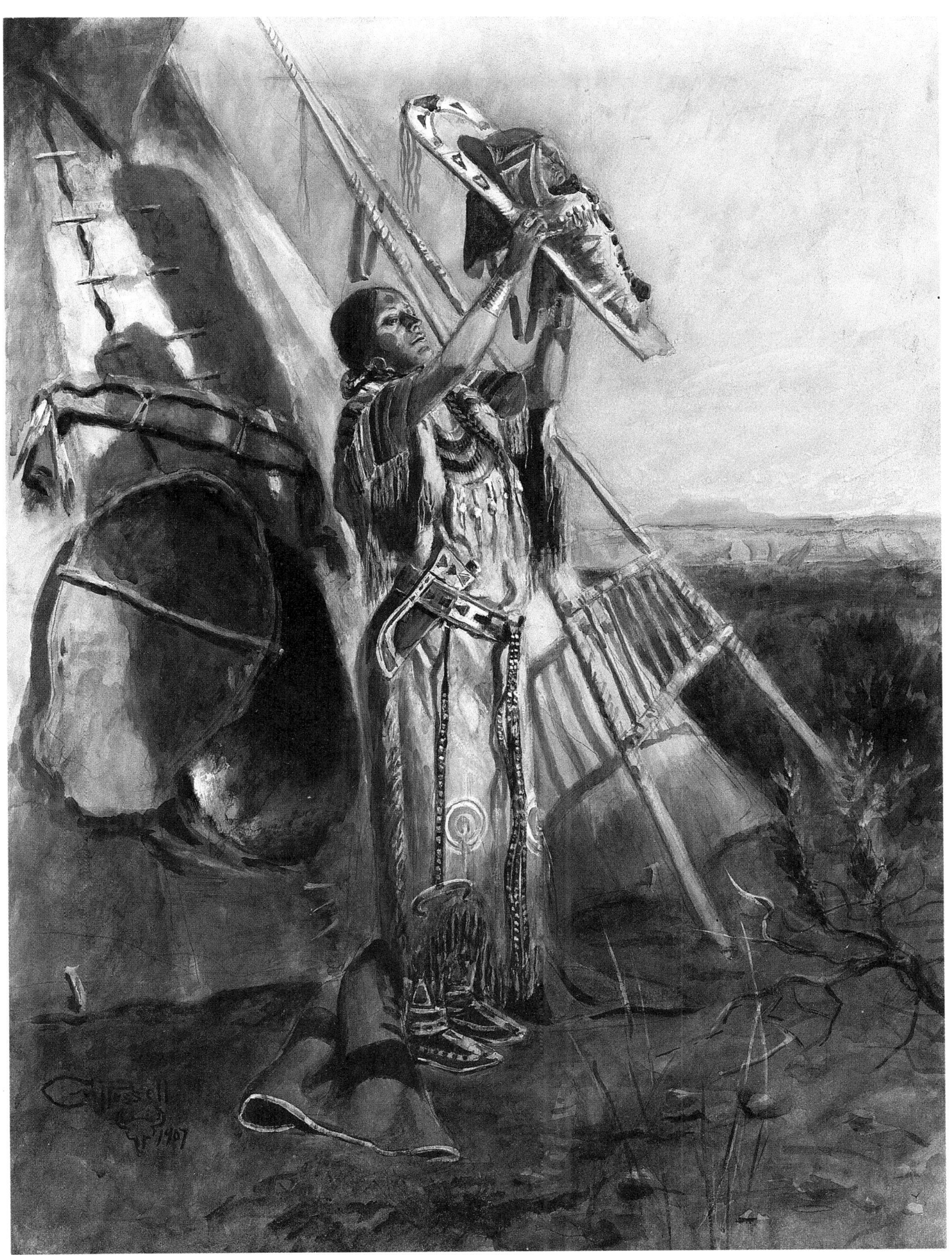

Sun Worship in Montana, 1907, gouache, watercolor, and graphite on paper

collection of Charles M. Russell's work in existence. Characteristically, he allowed the newly purchased collection to be exhibited at the Public Library and to used by the Fort Worth Art Association as a fund-raising opportunity.

Following Carter's death in 1955, tributes to his generosity and foresight poured in from all quarters, but there was more to come. On January 21, 1961, the doors of the Amon Carter Museum opened to the public for the first time, revealing an acclaimed collection of art to be enjoyed by future generations.

The Museum's founder intended the paintings of Charles M. Russell and Frederic Remington to be a lasting homage to the determination and courage of the pioneer spirit. "Amon G. Carter was born and reared in a frontier community," his old friend C. R. Smith wrote in the inaugural catalogue. "He acquired there the habits which later brought success to his business life. He also acquired and thereafter maintained a spirit of generosity. He wanted others to do well, he wanted to share with others the opportunities which come to able men."

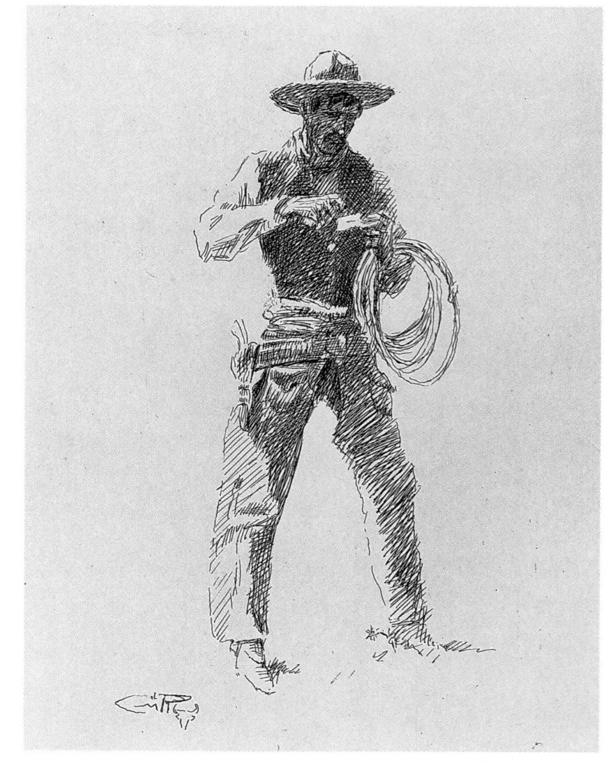

Making a Cigarette, 1911, pen and ink on paper

Friend Sid, 1914, watercolor, pen and ink, and graphite on paper

Opposite page:
Detail of *In Without Knocking*, 1909, oil on canvas

T.S. LINDER
GENERAL MERCHANT
THE HOFFMAN BAR
HO
LICENSED GAMBLING
$1000
REWARD
FOR
KID CURRY

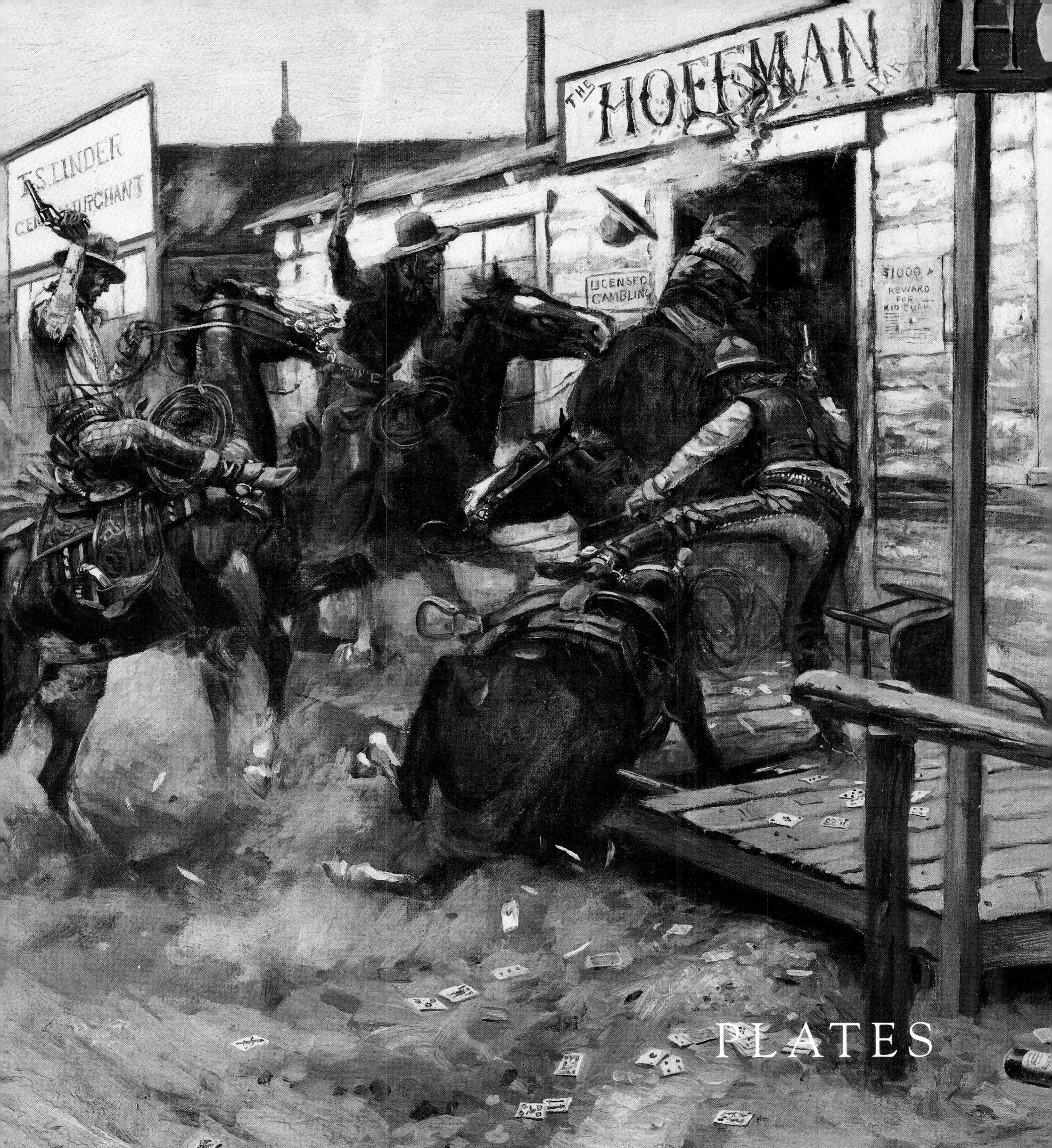

PLATES

Breaking Camp

c. 1885, oil on canvas, 18½ x 36¼ inches

When Charles M. Russell painted this view of an early morning in roundup camp, he was a twenty-one-year-old night herder in the Judith Basin country of central Montana Territory, and beginning to achieve a modest reputation as a painter of cowboy life on the open range. During his boyhood in Saint Louis, Russell had shown a strong aptitude for drawing and modeling, as well as an overwhelming desire to see the far western frontier. His great-uncles, Charles and William Bent, had been legendary figures on the old Santa Fe trail, but Russell's immediate family was less than encouraging. His father, having achieved prosperity himself, intended that his son join him in a business career. The young Russell persisted, however, and was finally allowed to travel to Montana with a family friend in 1880. His parents hoped that he would get the wanderlust out of his system, but in fact, the opposite happened; at not quite sixteen years of age, Russell first saw the land that he would call home for the rest of his life.

In 1880 Montana had not yet been traversed by railroads, and the Crow and Blackfeet Indian reservations occupied a large portion of the rolling plains east of the Rocky Mountains. Military forts still outnumbered settlements, and buffalo herds occasionally darkened the prairies. But profound changes already had occurred by 1885, when Russell probably painted *Breaking Camp*. The open-range cattle industry was at its zenith, and more than one million head roamed over the territory that had been opened, including the rich grasslands north and west of the Judith River.

Russell's painting depicts the cowboys in his outfit as they saddle their recalcitrant mounts from the remuda in the background. Some of the horses, their bellies full of tender prairie grass, are none too happy at the prospect of a tight cinch and a hard day's work. They vent their objections on the hapless riders, whose fellow cowhands cheer them on. Although a single buffalo skull occupies the right foreground—a melancholy reminder that those wild herds had already disappeared from the region—the overall celebratory flavor of this painting reveals Russell's love for the adventurous life he had adopted. Originally painted for Jesse Phelps, a fellow member of the roundup, it is one of the artist's earliest surviving efforts on canvas. It also became the first work to be exhibited outside Montana: Russell shipped it to Saint Louis for the 1886 Art Exposition. Perhaps unwittingly, he had launched his professional career as an artist.

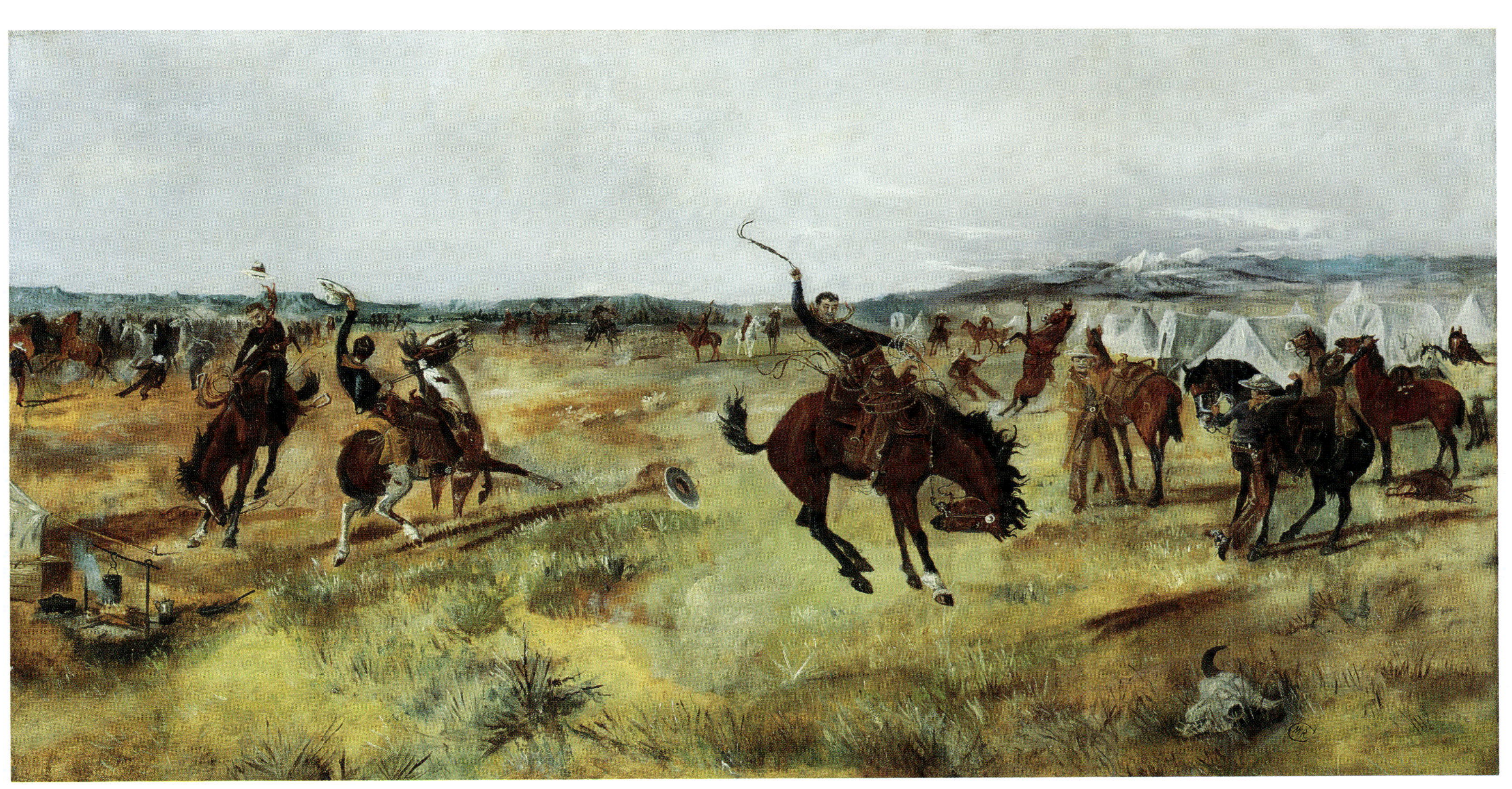

Cowboy Camp During the Roundup

c. 1885–87, oil on canvas, 23½ x 47¼ inches

Today the small town of Utica, Montana, near the Judith River and northeast of the Little Belt Mountains, rests amid fertile fields of wheat and other crops. A century ago, before the surrounding range was broken by the plow, Russell worked near there on annual roundups for a cattle syndicate. On January 12, 1887, the Fort Benton *River Press* noted that "while at Utica a River Press representative met Mr. Charles Russell, an artist of no ordinary ability. He has painted several of the most spirited pictures of cowboy life we have ever seen.... He is now engaged in painting a picture for James R. Shelton, in which are embraced the buildings of Utica, with a lively cowcamp in the foreground."

The resulting picture, *Cowboy Camp During the Roundup*, shows the whitewashed log buildings of the six-year-old settlement in the background, with Shelton's saloon on the left, his hotel in the center, and Hank Wright's post office and general store on the right. A blacksmith's shop is to the far left, while to the right a stagecoach following the old Carroll Trail between Lewistown and the mining camps drops into town.

In this period of his artistic life, Russell viewed his world as a folk artist and faithfully recorded every detail in a scene. A carefully fenced gravesite rests on the side of the hill behind the Shelton buildings—a detail the Sheltons insisted Russell include in the painting because it marked the resting place of their first-born daughter Esther, who died in 1885. In the foreground, Russell painted accurate likenesses of his fellow cowboys on the roundup, and many years later everyone still knew their identities. Henry Keeton, a lifelong friend of Russell's who recalled their roundup days together more than fifty years after the scene was painted, is supposedly the figure mounting his horse fifth from the left. In the lower right corner, Russell has again painted a buffalo skull lying in the grass just above his initials.

The painting tells a great deal about the cowboys' gear. Distinctive differences among their saddles revealed not only the origins of the riders but, to a larger extent, the mixture of cultural influences that marked the cowboy of the northern range. For example, the third horse from the left carries a finely tooled California saddle with pointed *tapaderos*. Keeton's saddle, on the other hand, is the more familiar Texas style, which was adapted by saddle-makers in Montana and Wyoming. A standing cowboy farther to the right attempts to control his bucking Appaloosa with a brightly striped rawhide reata, doubtless hand-made and highly prized. Russell, who acquired many articles of cowboy gear throughout his life, always kept his Cheyenne saddle, rawhide reatas, spurs, and "horse jewelry" that he had used in the Judith Basin.

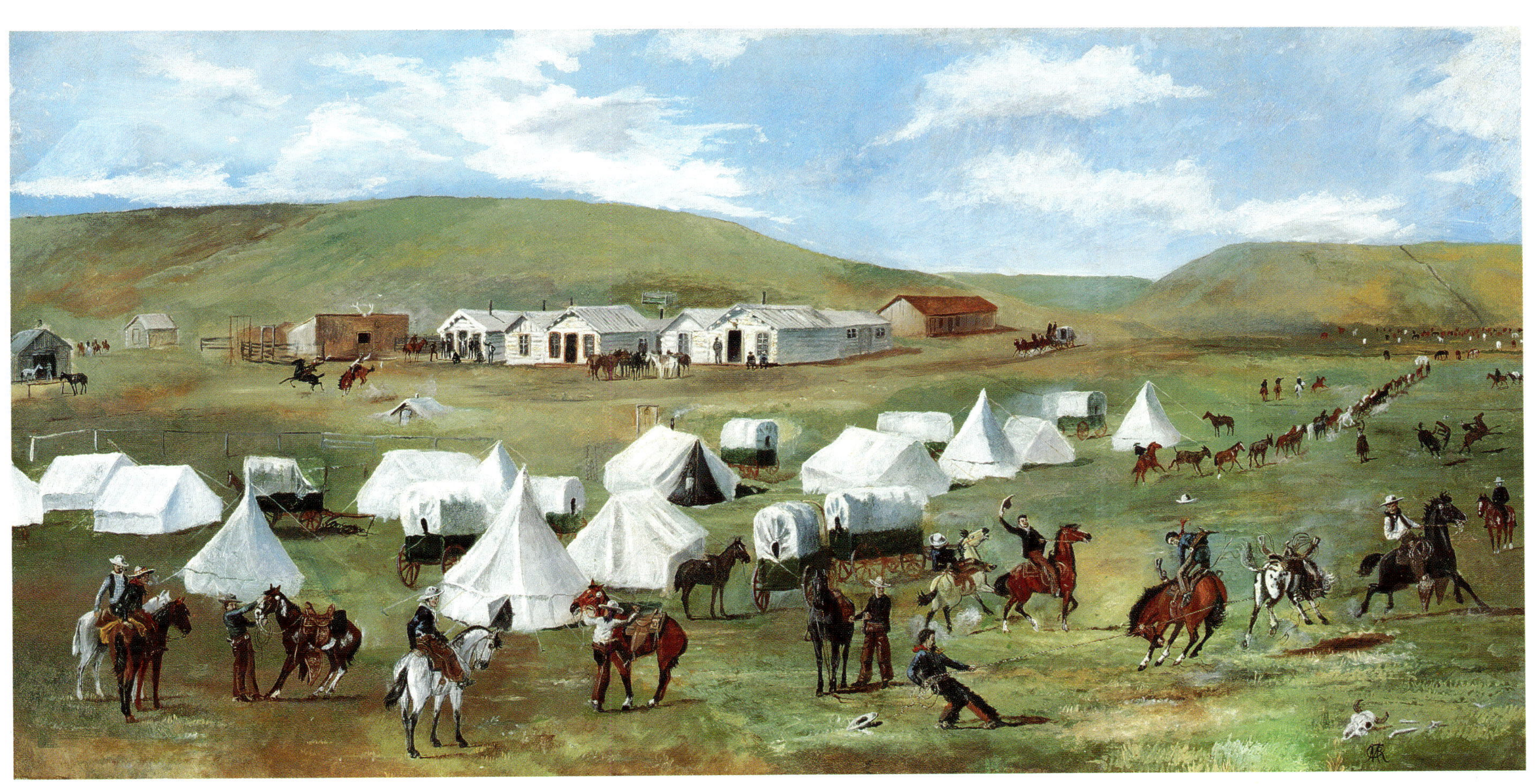

Lost in a Snowstorm—We Are Friends

1888, oil on canvas, 24 x 43⅛ inches

The winter of 1886–87, one of the most severe on record, broke the back of the Montana range cattle industry. Early snows, followed by a brief spell of warm weather, formed an impenetrable layer of ice over the grass. By January, temperatures had plummeted far below normal; howling blizzards marooned hundreds of cowboys away from their stock, and cattle died by the thousands. Russell was one of the stranded riders, and he sent his employers a grim message about the welfare of the herd with his now-famous watercolor of a single, starving cow menaced by hungry wolves in the snow. The subzero winter persisted until a chinook wind in early March carried away the cold and snow, revealing losses too great to comprehend for more than a year. Many stockmen lost between sixty and ninety percent of their entire herds. "Well we have had a perfect smashup all through the cattle country of the northwest," the usually indomitable Theodore Roosevelt wrote to a friend. "The losses are crippling. For the first time I have been utterly unable to enjoy a visit to my ranch. I shall be glad to get home."

Russell and his contemporaries knew well the dangers of a Montana winter. Winter travel posed great risks, particularly for those caught by a sudden storm in the open country. On many occasions, the weather was so intense that people lost their way between a ranch house and a nearby stable, and cowboys recalled that it was difficult to see their horses' heads in the driving snow, much less find their way to any destination. This is the subject of *Lost in a Snowstorm—We Are Friends*, where two mounted white men with a pack horse warily receive sign talk from a group of mounted Blackfeet Indians.

Although the Indians and white men remain guarded, the power of nature forces them to depend upon one another.

Russell has carefully rendered the myriad details of the Indians' dress, from their brightly colored trade blankets to the decorative beadwork of their rifle slings and bandoliers. The horses, all sensitively painted, turn their shaggy bodies against the bitter wind as one Indian makes the sign for "astride" to the lost cowboys. Russell's characteristic buffalo skull, soon to evolve into a schematized part of his signature, seems to disappear under the drifted snow. The painting obviously struck a responsive chord among Russell's audience, many of whom undoubtedly had heard accounts of being lost and narrowly escaping death in snowstorms.

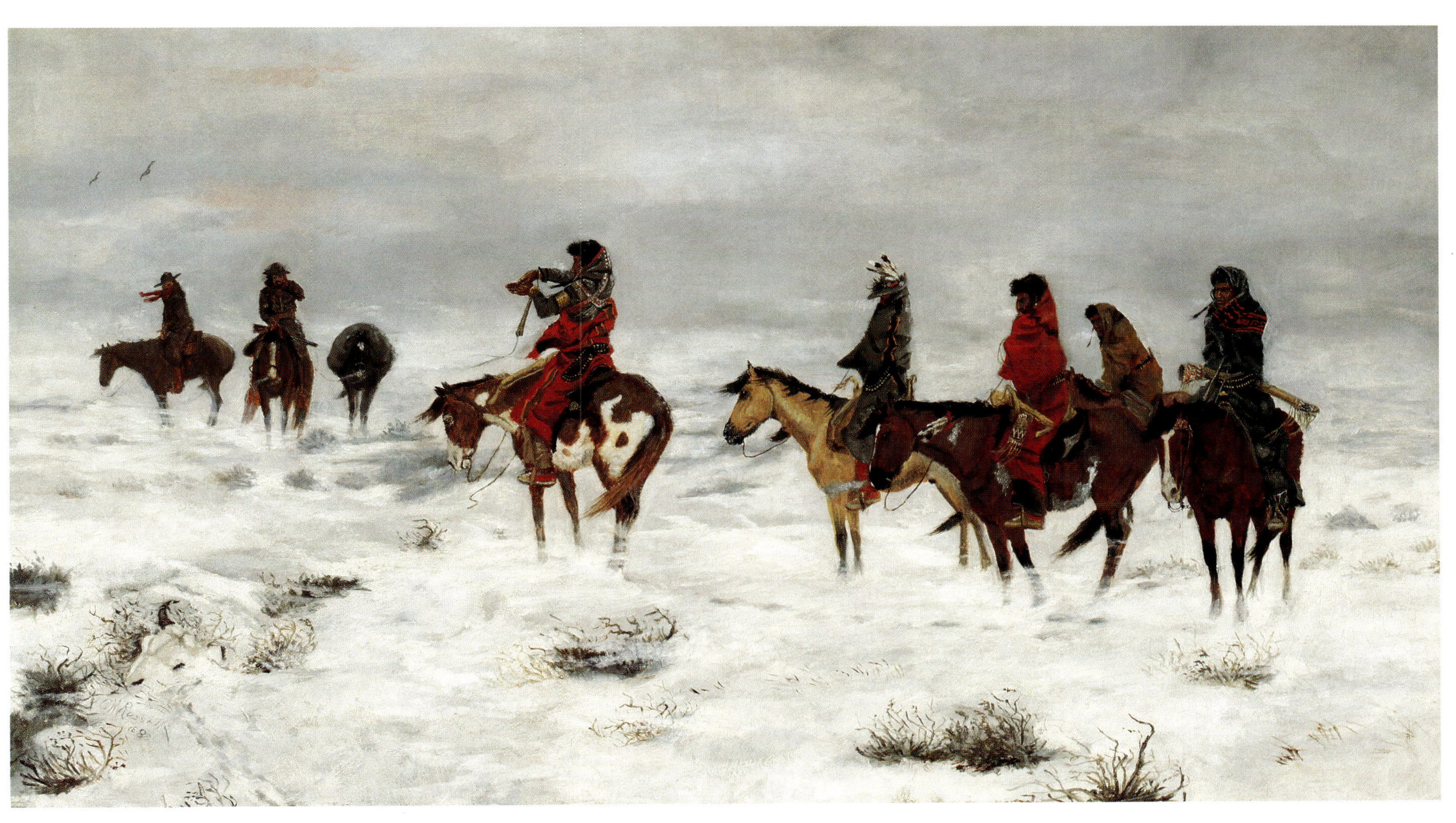

For Supremacy

1895, oil on canvas, 23⅛ x 35 inches

Although Russell gained early fame as "the Cowboy Artist," his depictions of the Northern Plains Indians represent some of his greatest achievements. Many accounts of Russell's life mention his extended stay among Alberta's Blood Indians in 1888 as a seminal influence on his artistic development, but it is more likely that his vision evolved through gradual, frequent contact with Indians as he traveled throughout the region over the years. In 1892, the Fort Benton *River Press* noted that Russell had a large collection of Indian artifacts, including clothing, weapons, and everyday items gathered from various places. He also knew the Indian sign language and throughout his life maintained friendships with individuals in several Montana tribes.

Russell must have realized soon after he arrived in Montana that the glory days of Plains Indian life, from the buffalo hunt to intertribal warfare, were gone forever. Nonetheless, there were many who could recall those fascinating events, and no doubt the young Russell listened intently. His artistic depictions of the Indians concentrated more and more on their adventurous life in the buffalo days, before there was much contact with white civilization.

Russell heard many accounts of intertribal warfare between the Blackfeet, Sioux, and Crow earlier in the century. Among the battles between Montana tribes was a bloody conflict in 1866, when the Piegan Blackfeet were said to have killed more than three hundred Crow and Gros Ventres near the Cypress Hills, exacting revenge for the murder of a prominent chief. Such conflicts usually involved a mounted charge into close combat, where warriors fought with bows, lances, clubs, and knives, and valor and victory were viewed as the sum of individual efforts. *For Supremacy* recounts such a pitched battle between two large parties.

Notable for its unflinching violence and vivid action, Russell's painting is also remarkable for its wealth of detail—from the painted buffalo robe on the fallen horse to the decorative beadwork objects that adorn the central figures. Northern Plains tribes had acquired horses in the mid-eighteenth century, and Russell accurately depicts the shortened bows that permitted greater accuracy on horseback. Russell's love of details ignores the fact that Indian warriors generally stripped down to the bare essentials for battle; objects such as a buffalo robe or beaded pipe bag would have been left behind.

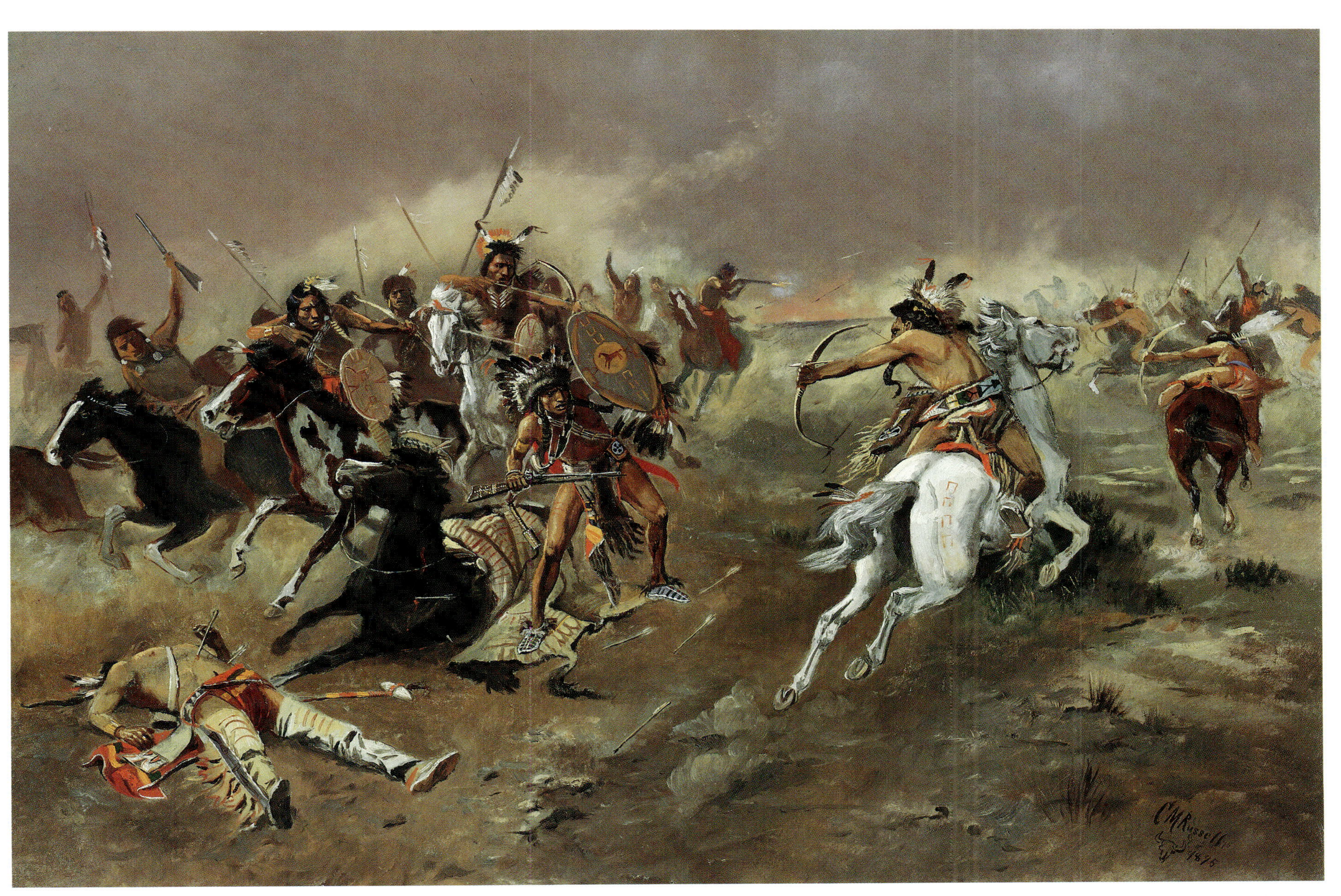

A *Doubtful Guest*

1896, watercolor, gouache, and graphite on paper, 18¾ x 22¾ inches

For the better part of his first two years in Montana Territory, Russell lived and worked with Jake Hoover, a skilled trapper, hunter, and erstwhile prospector who took the impressionable teenager under his wing. They lived in Hoover's cabin on the south fork of the Judith River in the Little Belt Mountains, and the young Russell worked as a cook, packer, skinner, and general helper. It seems possible that Hoover saw an echo of himself in the young Russell, for he also had come to Montana as a boy of sixteen. For Russell's part, he found a mentor who personified his ideal hero. Years later he recalled very simply, "This life suited me." It also gave the budding artist a deep understanding of nature and wildlife. As the two men rode a pack string mile after mile in all kinds of weather, Russell learned every corner of the region he would depict so vividly in paint.

The watercolor titled *A Doubtful Guest* is one of many autobiographical works the artist executed in later years to celebrate his youth on the frontier with a genuine mountain man. The painting shows Hoover reaching for his rifle as an Indian warrior steps into the clearing and holds his right arm aloft in a sign of peace. Russell himself wears the woven "half-breed" sash that would become a characteristic feature of his dress for the rest of his life. He grips his rifle in anticipation and warily prepares for the encounter.

Around the two men, Russell has arranged the objects of their camp. Dinner is being prepared on a campfire; a large pan, serving as a dutch oven, is propped up to bake some bannock, or flatbread. Nearby, the carcass of a freshly killed deer awaits skinning and butchering, probably for the main course. A pack saddle, carefully laid out, occupies the foreground. To the left, an animal skin has been staked out to dry, and a number of carefully detailed traps lie on the ground around Hoover's Indian-style frame saddle.

Russell's growing skill with the watercolor medium is readily apparent in this painting. The earthy, autumnal colors are washed and pooled to create shimmering effects of light and shadow, while details are rendered with more opaque and carefully controlled patches of color.

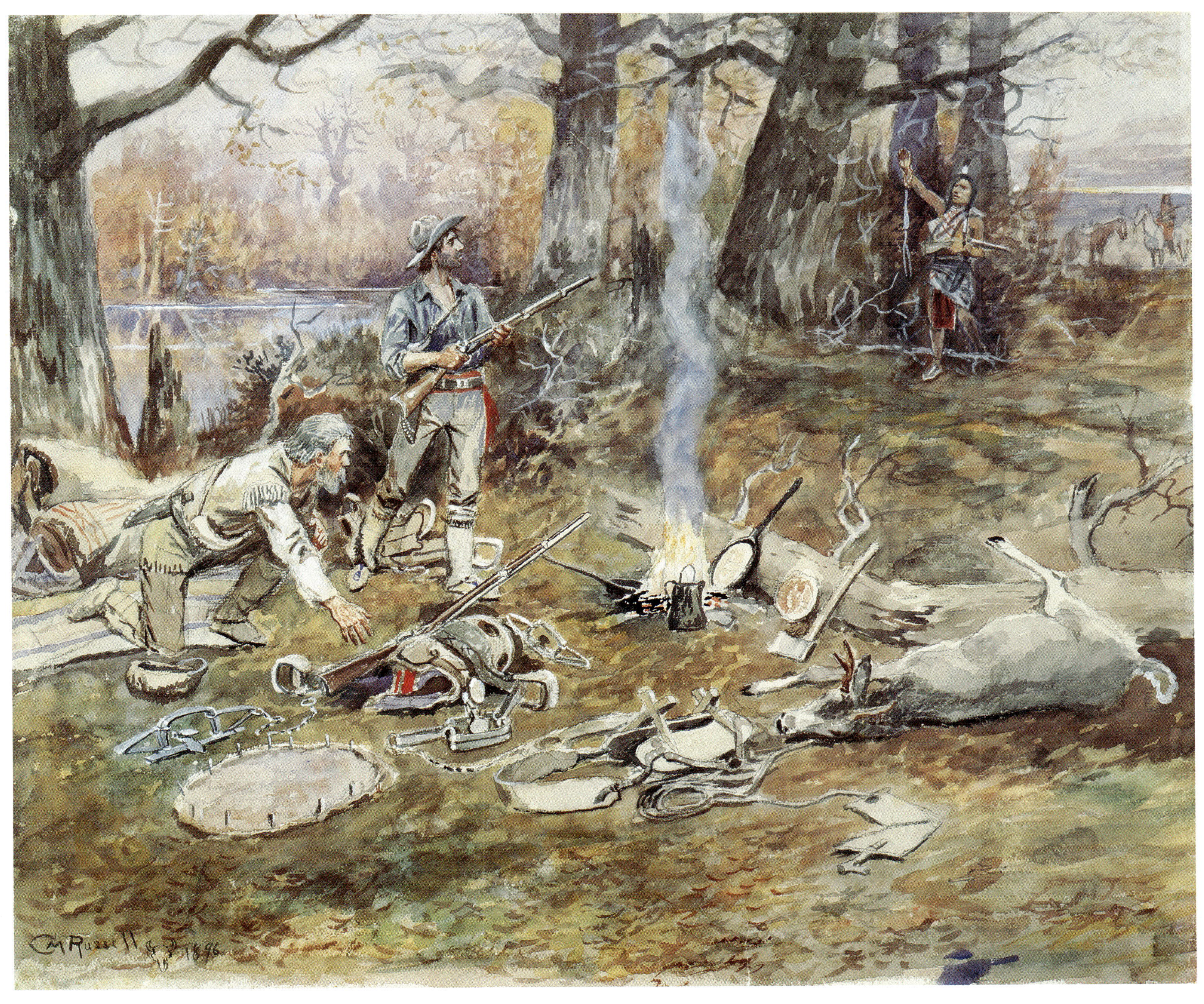
CMRussell 1896

A Piegan Flirtation

c. 1896, watercolor, gouache, and graphite on paper, 15 x 21¼ inches

Walter McClintock, who lived among the Blackfeet and recorded their customs at the time Russell painted this watercolor, wrote that marriage within the tribe "generally took place when a girl became about fourteen years of age, and sometimes as young as eight. If it happened that a young man fell in love with her, the proposal came from his parents. This, however, was unusual. It was not customary for unmarried girls to associate with men." Russell was fascinated by such everyday customs and events; few American artists approached his ability or desire to record every aspect of a culture he knew to be disappearing forever. *A Piegan Flirtation* sensitively portrays a somewhat surreptitious meeting between a young brave and an unmarried woman on the banks of a stream, away from the watchful eyes of the village. The young man on horseback regards the woman with a wonderful air of self-centered pride, while the woman turns coyly away, her expression a mixture of pleasure and amusement.

According to McClintock, if a woman and her parents accepted a suitor, her father made the proposal by saying that the girl would carry food to the suitor's lodge. If the man accepted this, she took food to him "for a moon," which constituted an engagement known to everyone in the village. Marriage rituals within the tribe were well established. The bride's family presented gifts to each member of the intended husband's family and arranged a feast for him and all his relatives. After the feast the man gave his future wife many presents to be distributed among her own family, while her mother prepared a new lodge stocked with blankets, robes, clothing, and other furnishings for the couple. Perhaps the most interesting aspect of a Blackfoot marriage was that the son-in-law never spoke to his mother-in-law, nor could she ever enter her daughter's lodge while he was there. "Even if he appeared unintentionally in her presence," McClintock wrote, "it was a breach of etiquette and placed her in such an embarrassing position, that he must make amends by presenting her with a horse."

The pencil lines of Russell's preliminary sketch for this painting are visible to the right and in the background. Overall, the watercolor technique shows the artist's increasing assurance and complexity, especially in the free strokes of the foreground foliage and the limpid washes of reflections on the water. Russell was naturally gifted as a watercolorist, and he came to prefer the medium's spontaneity and quickness.

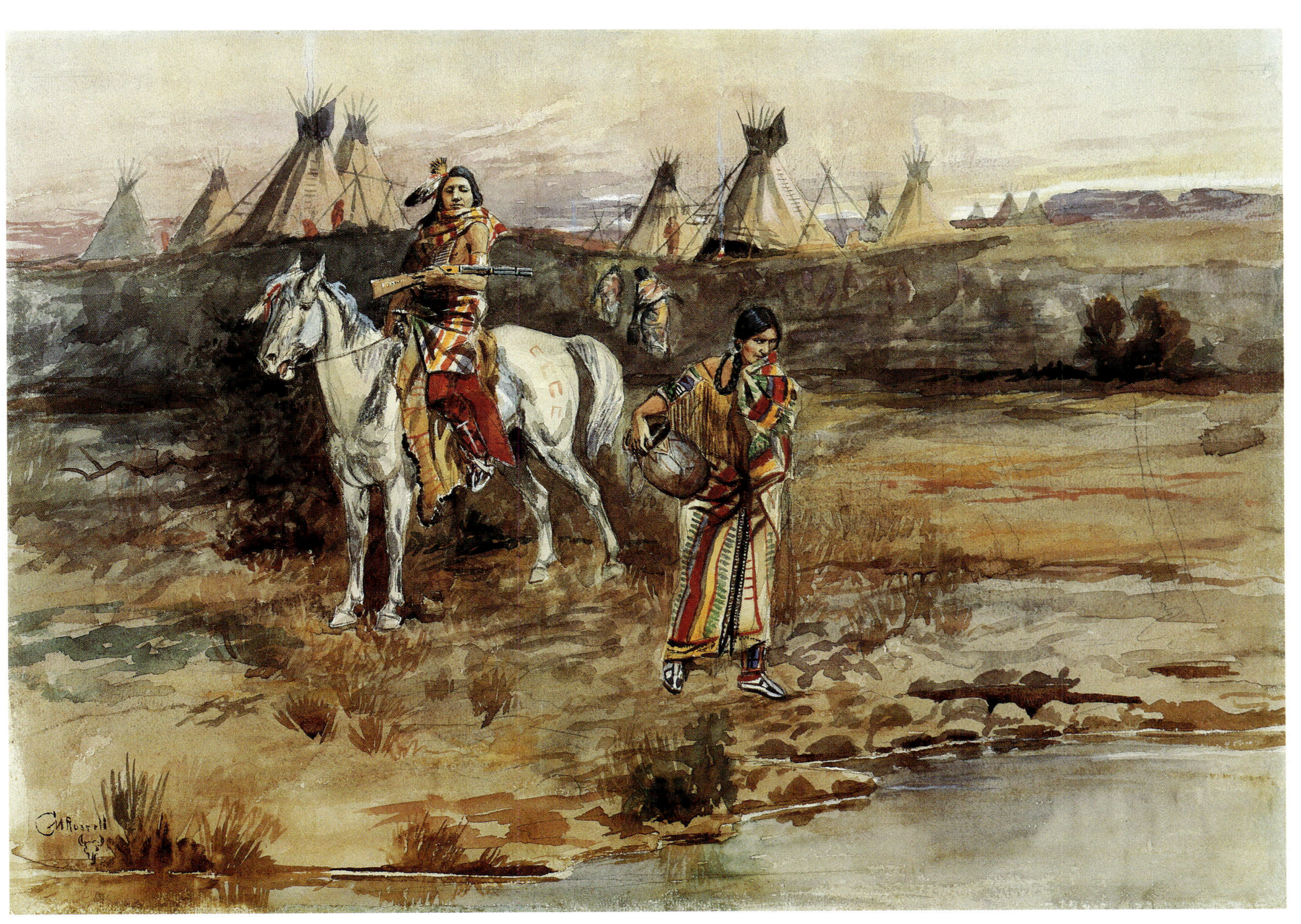

Squaws with Travois

1897, watercolor and graphite on paper mounted on board, 13¾ x 22¼ inches

The horse travois pictured here was a crucial item in the life of the Blackfeet. Oral tradition maintained that before the tribe acquired horses, dogs were outfitted with travois. As defined by ethnologist John C. Ewers, the true travois was an A-shaped drag, comprising two shafts made of lodgepole pine, with a loading platform and a hitch for attachment to the horse. The travois was made entirely of wood and rawhide. The poles, obtained from the eastern slopes of the Rockies or the Bear Paw Mountains, were about four to five inches wide at the base, slightly larger than lodgepoles. They were tied with a wet tendon from the back of a buffalo's neck, which was wrapped with a cover of soft-tanned skin. The apex allowed for no more than a three-foot projection, in order to maximize the "spring" of the poles. Generally, the poles were cut a little longer to allow for wear when they were dragged over the rough ground; even so, a travois often had to be replaced after a year's use. The hitch, visible as the decorated martingale above the horse's forelegs, was a flat strip of rawhide connected to two rawhide lines; the latter, about two fingers wide, were wrapped the length of the two poles to the lower part of the platform, where their ends were left long to tie loads. These lines, also visible in Russell's depiction, were crucial to the operation of the travois, carrying the weight of the load and preventing the poles from splitting. Contrary to what many writers have observed, the true travois is not to be confused with the improvised travois, which involved a makeshift platform tied to bundles of lodgepoles.

As this vibrant watercolor suggests, the travois was made and owned by the women of the tribe and used for a number of tasks that involved transporting people (such as children, invalids, or the aged) or the materials of camp, such as robes and bedding. The women referred to the hitch as "my load" and the platform as "my broad road." When not being used for travel from one campsite to another, as depicted in the watercolor, the travois had a variety of other practical purposes, such as a ladder for the women to erect or disassemble the lodges, or a framework for drying meat.

The Indian woman in Russell's watercolor has paused with her young son to allow the horses to drink. The decorated cradle which hangs from the front saddle horn was a luxury item among the Blackfeet; most women carried their babies on their backs, wrapped in skins or robes. A large skinning knife, with its tack-studded sheath, can be seen on her belt, and she holds an elkhorn-handled quirt in her right hand.

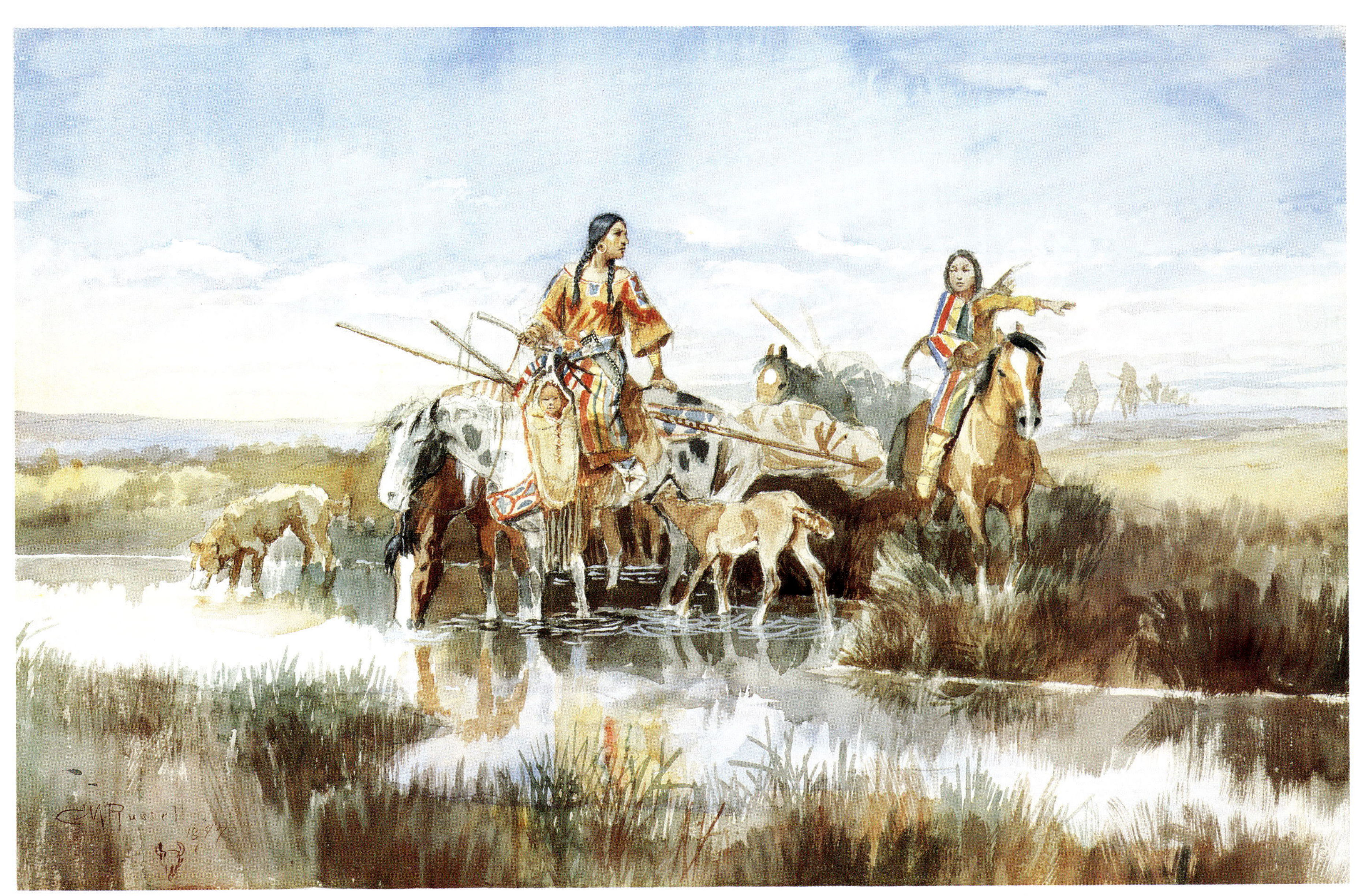

Bronc in Cow Camp

1897, oil on canvas, 20⅛ x 31¼ inches

One bright spring day in May 1897, William Cameron, a young editor for a new sportsman's magazine titled *Western Field and Stream*, paid a visit to Russell and his bride, Nancy Cooper Russell, at their one-room home in Cascade, a small town southwest of Great Falls. Cameron was interested in commissioning a number of paintings for the magazine, and he was thrilled to be invited to visit the studio and watch Russell paint. Recalling his memorable visit more than fifty years later, Cameron wrote: "He took out his little bag of Bull Durham and holding the tie string in his teeth rolled himself a cigarette before sitting down to continue painting." Cameron described the picture on the easel as a spirited scene in a roundup camp, where a cow pony was objecting to a cold saddle on its back by "bucking a hole in the cook's nice breakfast fire." This was probably *Bronc in Cow Camp*, the painting pictured here. Russell "seemed to be enjoying himself," Cameron remembered, adding that "he evidently had the scene clearly mapped out in his mind."

Russell painted more than one version of this subject, each one referring to a particular story he had heard. This painting depicts the predicament of one of Russell's friends, Robert "Corduroy Bob" Thoroughman, as his ornery pinto scatters the campfire and various cooking pots across the ground. The exasperated cook, with shovel upraised, is about to give Thoroughman's mount an additional brand on his backside. Russell loved hearing such stories of the cow camps, particularly those told by the riders on themselves.

Thoroughman was one of the first settlers in the Chestnut Valley, where Cascade is located. This incident was said to have occurred in 1879, and the misbehaving pinto was apparently an Indian pony. According to family accounts, Thoroughman was working for an outfit called Sands and Taylor, whose monogram is visible on the tent to the left, as they drove a large herd of twenty-seven hundred cattle to the Teton country. Thoroughman probably also told Russell about the Indians stealing a number of their horses during the drive. The cowboys pursued them, and in the battle that followed, lives were lost on both sides, although the cowboys recovered their horses. In April 1920 Russell wrote Thoroughman about "the kind of men that brought the spotted cattle to the west before the humped-back cows were gone." He added that "most of these people live now only in the pages of history but they were regular men Bob and you were one of them."

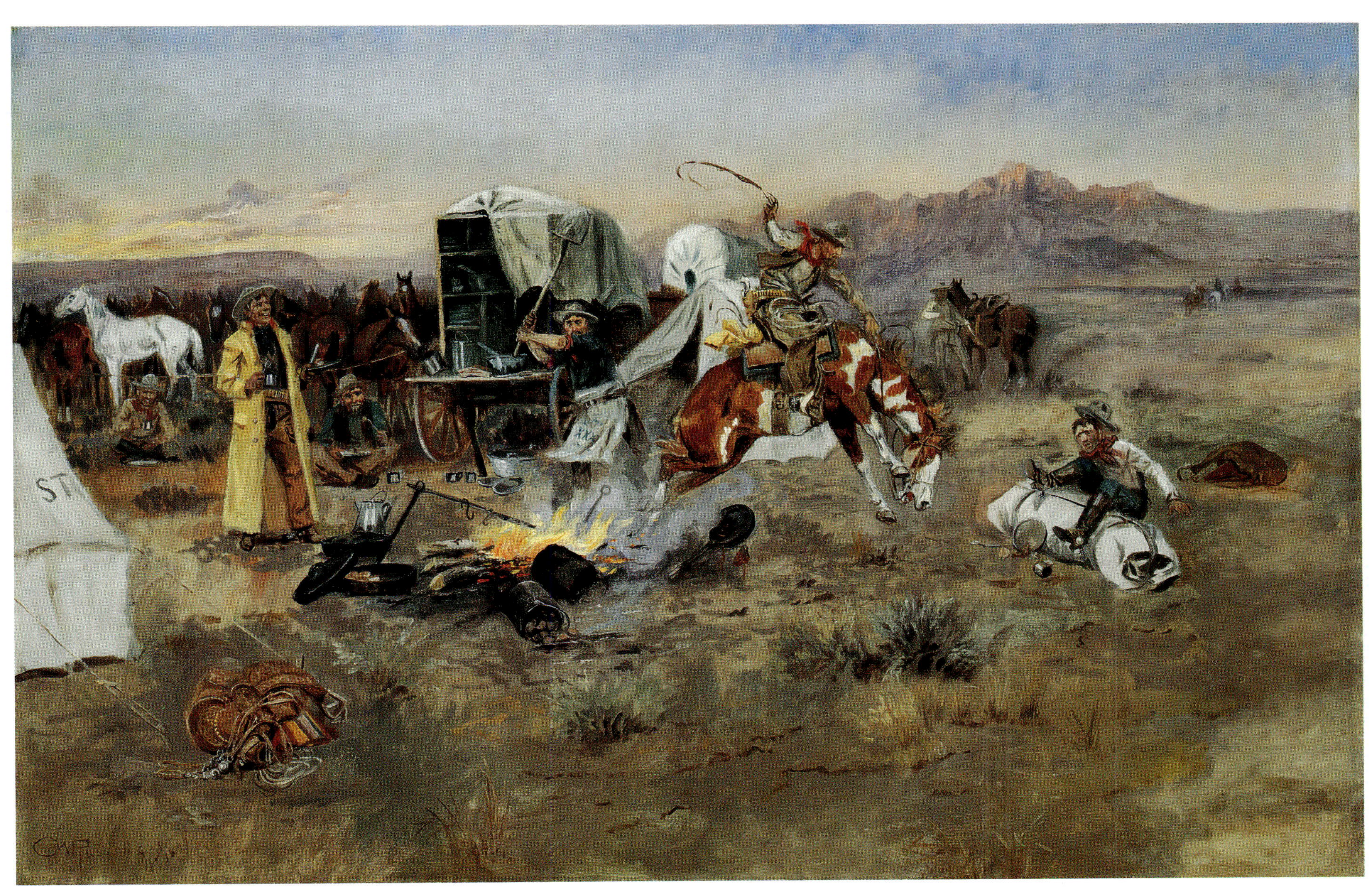

The Hold Up

1899, oil on canvas, 30⅛ x 48⅛ inches

With the arrival of the transcontinental railroads in frontier towns and booming mining centers, the overland stagecoach routes shifted to smaller feeder lines that provided passenger and freight service to outlying locations. One of the most famous of these was the Cheyenne-Black Hills route, established in the late 1870s following the Custer massacre and the repudiation of the Sioux Treaty. The stage route helped to open the Black Hills area to settlement and to exploitation of its rich gold reserves. As stagecoaches starting transporting great wealth from the mines around Deadwood, bands of outlaws began frequenting the three-hundred-mile stretch of the trail to rob them. The banditry soon reached an unparalleled level, only to be sharply curtailed in 1880 by stringent law enforcement measures and vigilante justice by outraged citizens.

Russell heard many memorable accounts of the highwaymen, for the stories were extensively recorded in the newspapers and widely repeated throughout the region.

The painting depicts the Deadwood stagecoach after it has been halted by "Big Nose George" Parrott, a well-known real-life outlaw. Parrott, his prominent nose silhouetted behind a black mask, aims his gun at the lined-up passengers while a cohort frisks them. The characters in Russell's stagecoach are a catalogue of western stereotypes: the frontier preacher, the pretty young woman and her elderly escort, the dapper mustachioed gambler, the Chinese immigrant, the Jewish merchant. Although some are racial caricatures, they were part of a common language in Russell's day. The scene seems to have inspired a host of western movies, among them John Ford's epochal *Stagecoach*, released in 1939 and starring a young John Wayne.

As for Big Nose George, the law caught up with him after he attempted to rob a Union Pacific train. He and his gang were captured by a posse and jailed in Rawlins, Wyoming, to await trial. While in jail, Parrott attempted an escape, seriously wounding a jailer before his efforts were foiled by the jailer's wife. Soon after, on an April night in 1880, an enraged crowd stormed the jail, carried Parrott off, and hanged him from a telegraph pole. A grisly coda to the story, reported in the *Rocky Mountain Husbandman* in 1933 and 1934, suggests that a local doctor removed portions of the outlaw's skin, which was then tanned to make a variety of objects, including a purse and a pair of ladies' shoes.

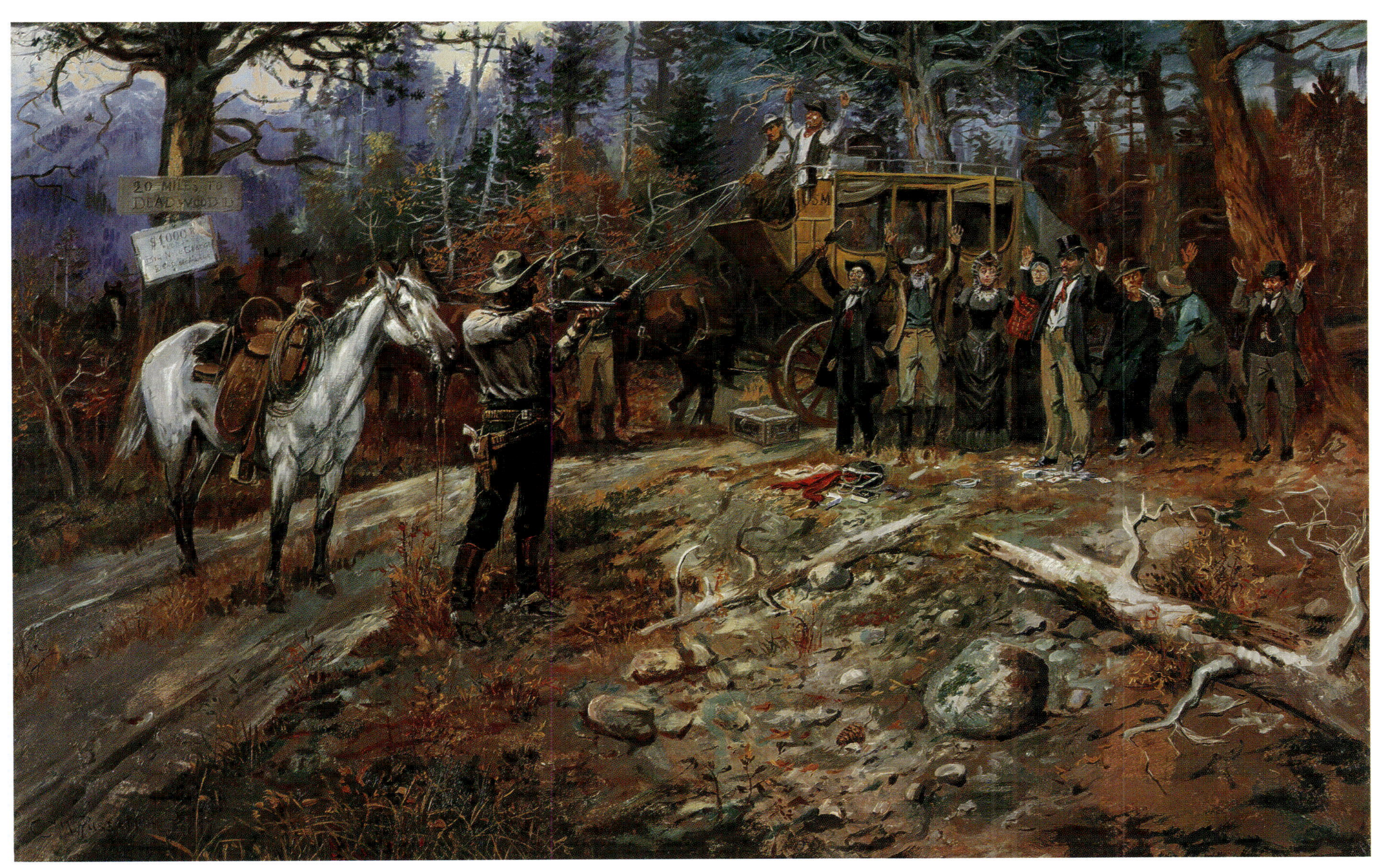
20 MILES TO
DEADWOOD
$1000

Buffalo Hunt No. 26

1899, oil on canvas, 30⅛ x 48⅛ inches

In his lifetime, Russell depicted the Indian buffalo hunt more than any other subject. He was fascinated by this legendary contest between man and animal, and he realized that it represented, perhaps more than anything else could, the spirit of the wild frontier that was gone forever. Russell arrived in Montana Territory after the great buffalo herds had dwindled to a handful of smaller ones; by 1884, these too were mostly gone. He learned many details of the buffalo hunt from his Blackfeet acquaintances, but he also was familiar with the work of several of his artistic predecessors in the area, most notably George Catlin and Carl Wimar. Russell owned copies of Catlin's books, which described in vivid detail the buffalo hunts by the Plains Indians in the 1830s, and he used Catlin's eyewitness accounts and accompanying depictions as raw material for his own work. He thought Catlin's art lacked polish, but he had no such reservations about the work of Carl Wimar, a fellow Saint Louis artist who, in 1859, had traveled up the Missouri River as far as Fort Benton. Russell viewed Wimar's work whenever he went back to Saint Louis; one of his favorite paintings was a large buffalo hunt that Wimar had painted for a local patron in 1861. Russell kept a photograph of this painting in his studio, doubtless for inspiration rather than as a direct source. To an early Wimar biographer he wrote, "I have always liked his work and think he knew the Indian."

Russell's powerful painting echoes Catlin's description of Indian buffalo-hunting techniques. The hunters, having cut off part of a herd, are attacking from two directions and forcing the frightened animals to turn into each other—a technique that minimized the danger of the riders being gored or trampled. On the left, a highly trained "buffalo horse" surges up to the right of one animal and, in Catlin's words, gives "his rider the chance to throw the arrow to the left, which he does at the instant the horse is passing—bringing him opposite the heart, which receives the deadly weapon 'to the feather.'" On the right, a mounted warrior is set to drive his lance into another beast, which recoils into the charging group. Russell's depiction of the scene is relatively accurate, except for the absence of saddles, which many Blackfeet maintained were used in the hunt for obvious reasons of safety and stability.

The surrounding landscape resembles the Sun River country along the front range of the Rockies. In the foreground, a clump of sagebrush conceals a rattlesnake that is likely very excited by all the commotion.

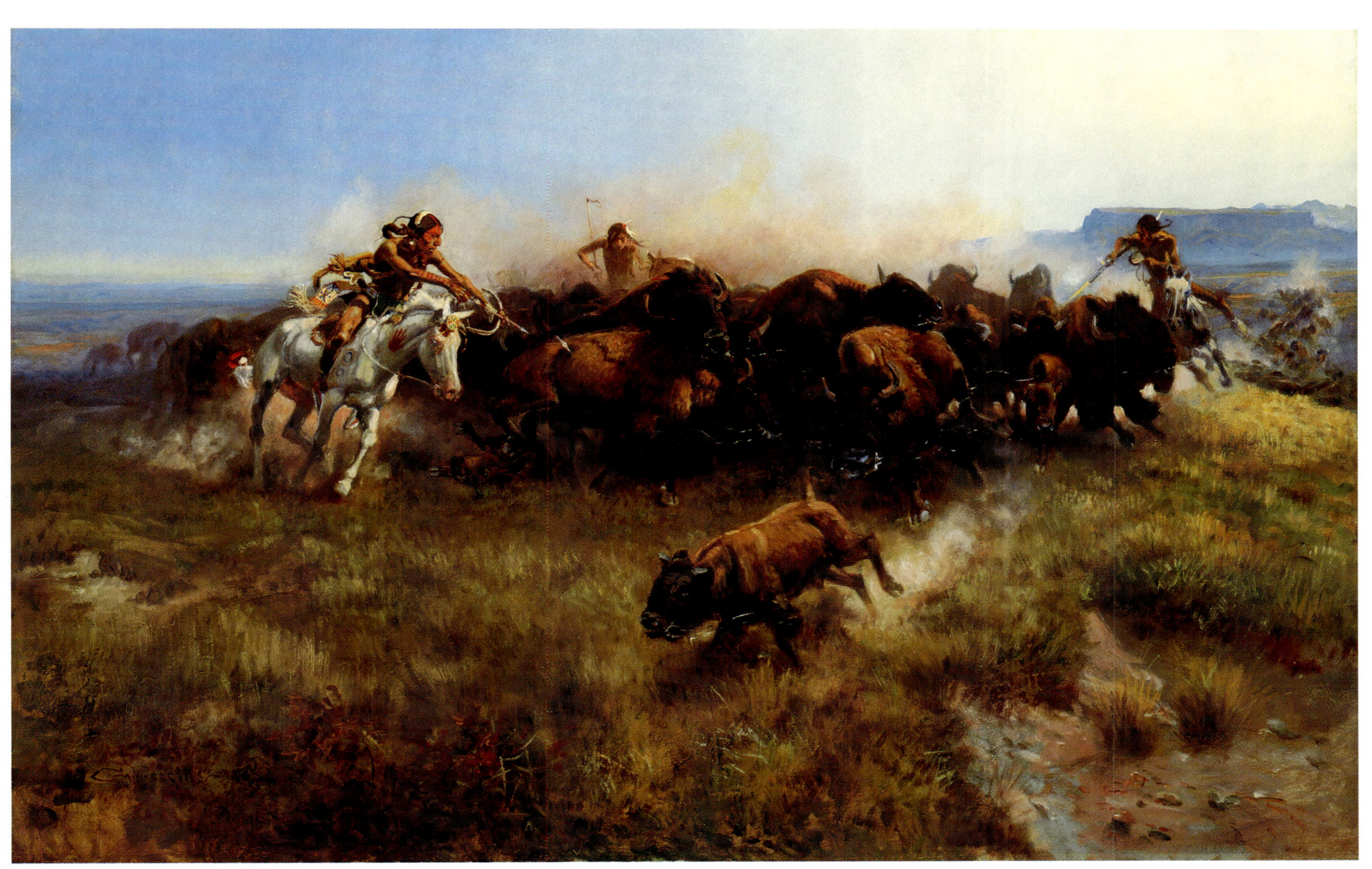

The Horse Thieves

1901, oil on canvas, 24 x 30 inches

Horse raiding was the most common type of war expedition among the Blackfeet. Several writers reported the activity, and some claimed that as many as twenty raids on a single tribe were made within a year. After the Indians were confined to reservations, the practice still remained a volatile threat to inter-tribal peace. Russell's painting is again based on the legendary exploits of a historical figure: White Quiver, a Piegan warrior who was remembered as the greatest horse raider of his time and was still active when Russell executed this portrayal. The painting doubtless was based on the many stories of the warrior's remarkable career.

White Quiver was a young boy when his father, Trail's War Bonnet, was killed by the Crow. Vowing vengeance on that tribe, the son joined war parties while young and developed into a warrior of great physical prowess. It was said that he could ride three days and nights with stolen horses without stopping for food. He was described as tall, very dark, and ugly; he became so well known to the enemy tribe that Crow mothers disciplined their misbehaving children with threats of his stealthy presence. White Quiver's war parties were small ones, and as Russell accurately shows, he was always the leader. He developed the unorthodox practice of entering an enemy camp alone, at dusk, just as the people were settling down for the night, then bringing the horses out to the other members of his party. He took horses from other tribes besides the Crow, including the Assiniboine, Cree, Gros Ventres, and Sioux.

In Russell's painting, White Quiver leads a large band of stolen horses, under cover of darkness, from a river bottom up into the high country. He wears a wolfskin war bonnet with a single eagle feather. It was said that his "power" came from a single plume obtained from an Arapaho medicine pipe bundle.

During his last raid, when he was thirty, White Quiver stole more than fifty horses from the Crow. Military authorities from Fort Benton intercepted him and took the horses, but after dark, he restole them from the government corrals and drove them quickly into Canada. There the Mounted Police stopped him and again confiscated the horses. Again White Quiver got part of the herd back and took them to the Blackfeet reservation in Montana. As in every raid he led, White Quiver distributed the horses to friends and relatives, keeping only a few for himself. Such exploits earned him the accolades of a popular hero, as well as a place in Russell's art.

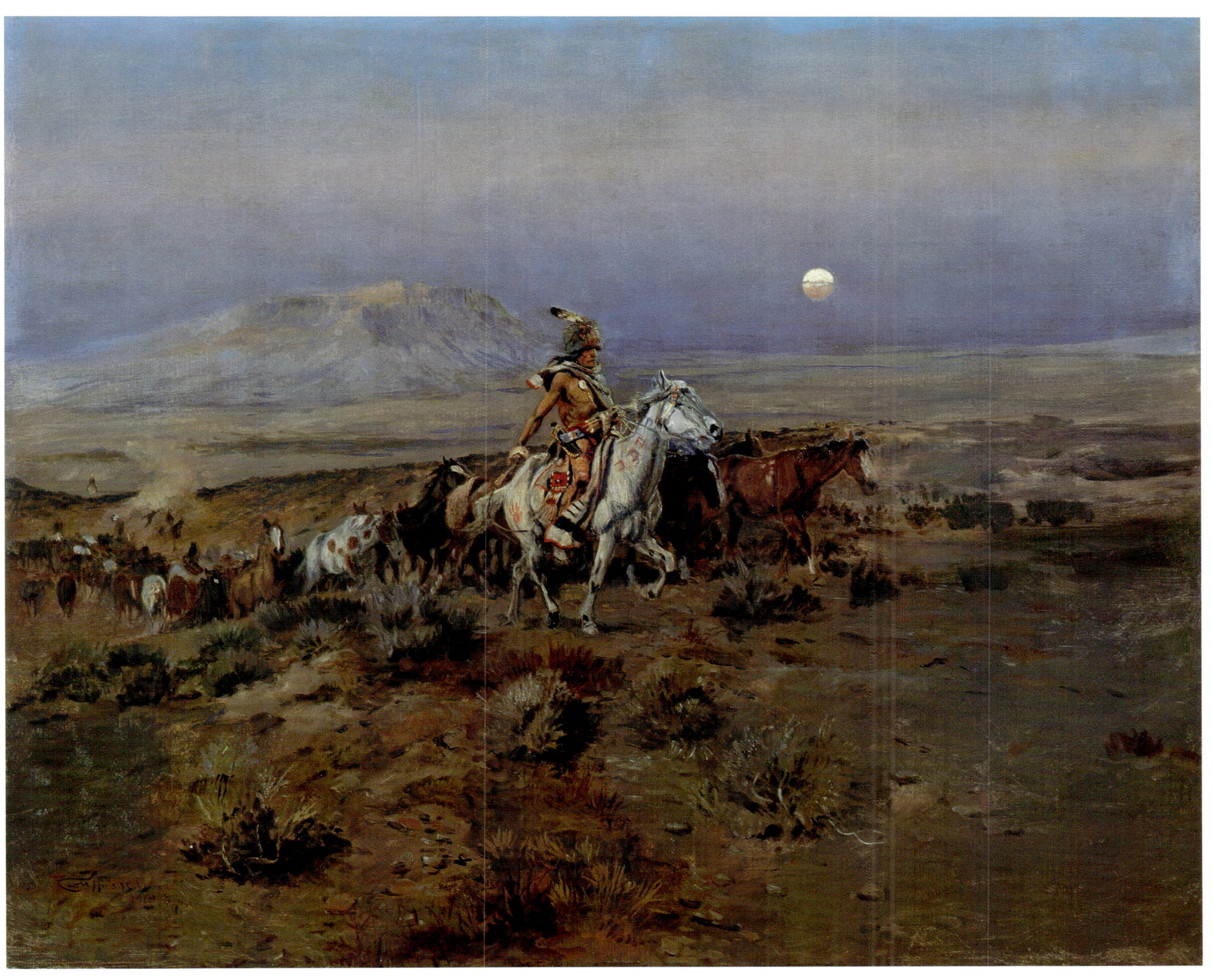

Christmas at the Line Camp

1904, gouache, watercolor, and graphite on paper, 18⅞ x 23⅞ inches

"Winter work does not require as many hands as are needed in other seasons," Fay Ward wrote in his book, *The Cowboy at Work.* "The old hands—men who have made good—are the ones who are generally given a winter job. Gathering poor cows, cutting ice to open up water holes, feeding bulls and poor stock, hauling firewood, and riding line to keep stock from drifting off their range are the things which keep a stockhand from getting lonesome in the winter." Each cowhand used at least two "winter" horses, strong mounts that could support a rider and a weakened calf while also driving a cow.

Some of the winter hands performed their duties from a line camp, which was usually located on the outer edge of the outfit's range. Such places were very isolated, as Russell has shown in this accomplished watercolor. Two riders, possibly from the home ranch, have ridden through the bitter cold to greet two cowboys who emerge from a log line shack. The visitors have brought what must be a welcome Christmas repast—a freshly killed antelope. Russell has employed gouache (opaque watercolor) to evoke the stark whiteness of the wintry landscape, then touched it with washes of pale color. He gives both men and horses visible clouds of breath, indicating deep cold as well as an unfriendly wind. The lead rider wears a sourdough coat, a heavy canvas garment that was often lined with wool fleece, as well as woolly chaps to keep out the cold. On the wall of the cabin, two freshly dressed wolf skins reveal another activity that the line camp hands performed—keeping roving predators away from the vulnerable stock.

Life in a line camp must have been hard, particularly in bad weather. The wood in front of the shack indicates the sole source of heat inside, and one may imagine how frigid these places became when the temperatures dipped well below zero and the winds howled from the north. The danger of severe frostbite was all too real; many cowhands in Russell's day had parts of their fingers or toes missing to prove it. One writer recalled his brief visit to a line shack in the bitter cold. As the men tried to fire up the small stove, one of the hands said, "The worst thing in the world for us right now would be a lot of heat. If you think freezing up's hell, wait till you try thawing out too fast." That day in the line shack, the men were unable to read their own thermometer. "Ours only registers down to thirty below," one of the cowhands explained. "This here must be a tropical model."

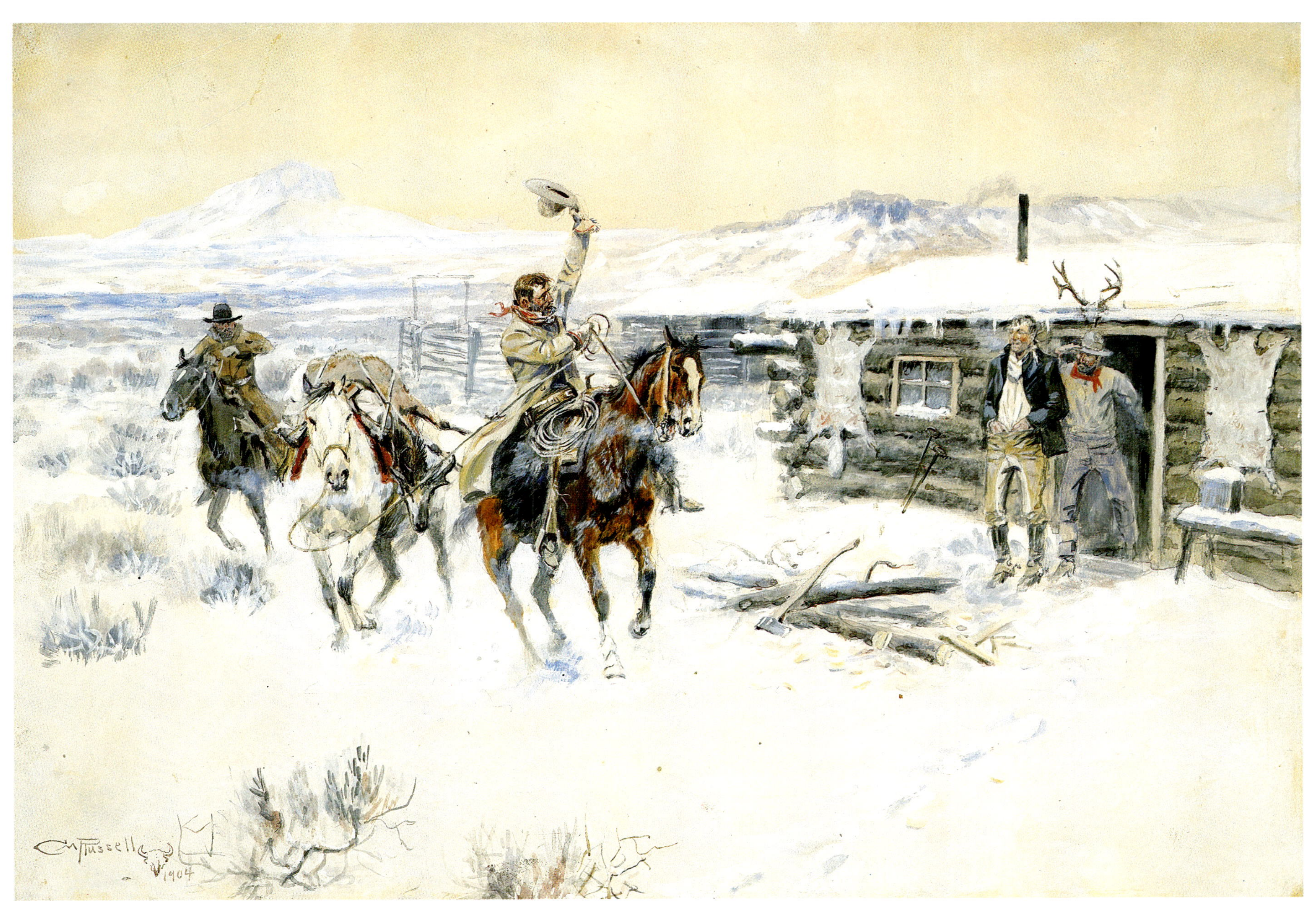

Lewis and Clark on the Lower Columbia

1905, gouache, watercolor, and graphite on paper, 18¾ x 23⅞ inches

As Russell's art developed and he began to receive more commissions as an illustrator, he steeped himself in the history of the West. Throughout his life he was captivated by the exploits of the Lewis and Clark expedition, and by the time of the expedition's centennial observances in 1904 and 1905, Russell had already executed a number of Lewis and Clark subjects and had familiarized himself with published versions of their journals. This evocative watercolor of a true event, executed a century after the expedition, shows the explorers meeting a group of Indians in decorated dugout canoes somewhere on the lower Columbia River.

Towards the end of October 1805, Lewis and Clark proceeded into the Cascade region of the Columbia, where the river passed through the mountain range of the same name. On October 23, at an Indian village along the river, William Clark observed a new type of canoe, "wide in the middle and tapering to each end, on the bow curious figures were cut in the wood." The canoes were stronger and better-crafted than the ones the expedition already possessed, so Captain Lewis managed to purchase one for the journey downstream. Passing the falls around the present-day town of The Dalles, the party entered the territory of the Chinookan-language Indian tribes.

Russell's watercolor could easily depict the "cool windy morning" on the river that Clark described on October 28, when the party encountered three canoes from upriver, filled with Indians who had come to observe them. Clark noted that the Indian canoes were "built of white cedar or pine[,] very light…with aperns, and heads of animals carved on the bow, which is generally raised." Russell has shown Clark standing at the stern of his canoe, his characteristic red hair barely visible under his cap, attentively cradling his rifle while observing the visitors. Sacajawea, the expedition's Shoshone guide, attempts to talk sign language with the Indians—a bit of artistic license since it is doubtful they would have understood her. Below her Russell has painted York, Clark's Negro manservant, whose dark skin fascinated the Indians. Misty clouds hang on the water, shrouding the dark forms of the conifer-covered landscape. To reinforce the mood, Russell effectively bathes the whole scene in light purples, pale blues, and rosy pinks.

At this point in his life, Russell had never seen the lower Columbia. It is likely that he derived his knowledge of the elaborate headdresses, decorated clothing, and design motifs on the Indian canoes from objects he had recently seen in George Heye's extensive collection in New York City. They are all typical of Indian tribes found farther north, in British Columbia.

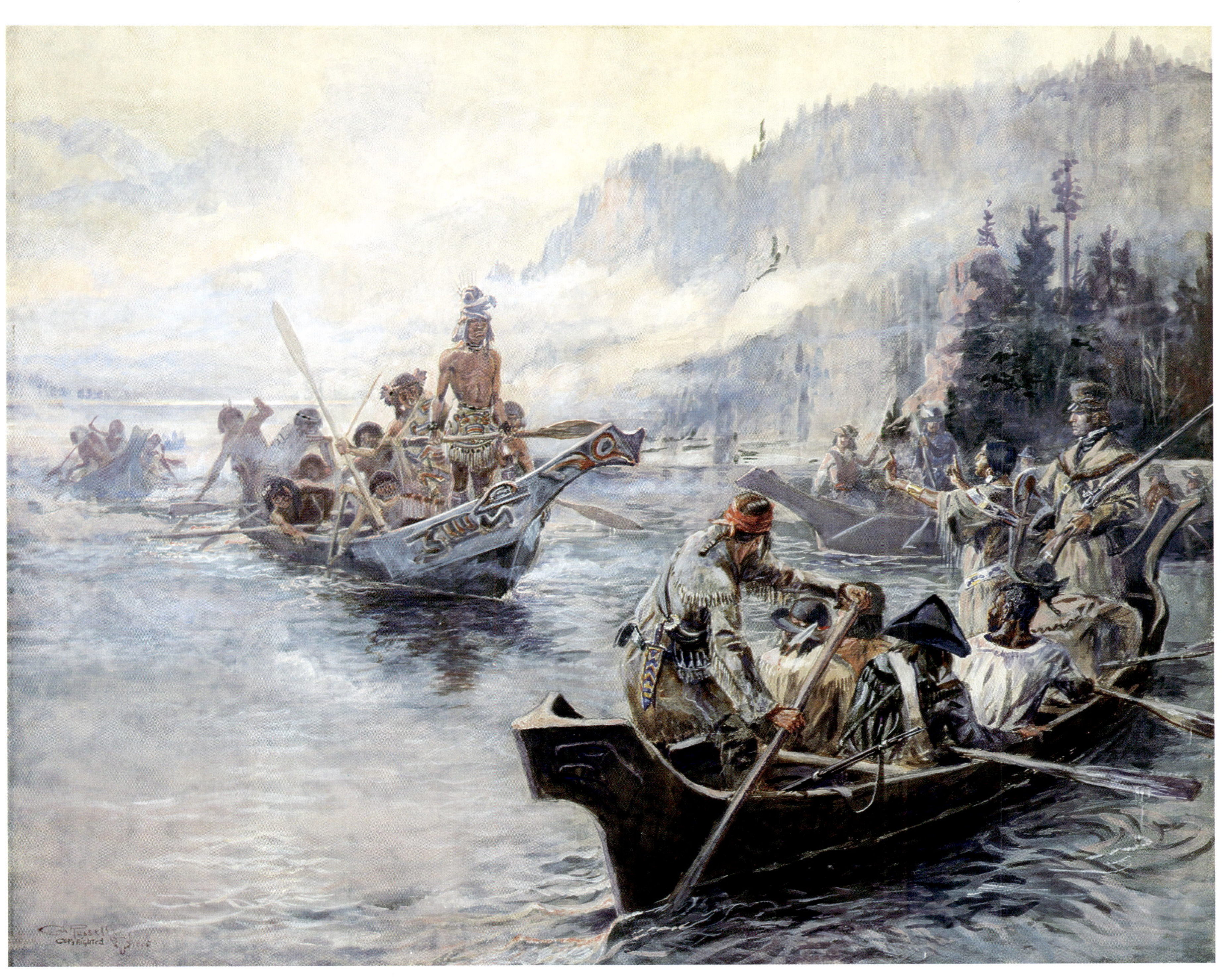

The Wolfer's Camp

1906, gouache, watercolor, and graphite on paperboard, 14¾ x 20⅞ inches

This wintry scene appeared in the December 13, 1906, issue of *Leslie's Weekly* under the title, "The Red Man's Christmas Gift." The actual subject doesn't have much to do with Christmas, nor is it likely the Indian intends the freshly killed antelope to be a gift. He seems to be making the sign for "done" or "end," indicating that he has just concluded a trade between himself and a cowboy in a canvas sourdough coat, who stands with his back to a roaring campfire.

The cowboy wears typical gear of the 1880s: Montana peak hat, Mexican loop holster with an ivory-handled six-shooter, one-piece stovepipe-top boots, and dropshank spurs. His partner squats behind the fire, skillet in hand, while bread bakes in another pan propped to face the heat. The Indian is warmly dressed in animal-skin garments, a Pendleton trade blanket wrapped around his leggings. His coat is animal skin with the hair on the inside for warmth and comfort. The Indian's wife and child stand behind him; although wrapped snugly in brightly patterned Pendleton blankets, they appear chilled. Russell has correctly shown a pad saddle on the warrior's horse and a woman's "wood saddle," with its characteristically high pommel and cantle, on the other. The white man's saddle and pack saddle lie on the snow in the foreground, while another saddle hangs from a tree.

In the background, four wolf pelts are strung on a line running from the hunters' tent. Cattlemen of Russell's day saw the wolf as the ultimate villain, and Russell himself seems to have accepted this attitude. With the disappearance of the buffalo, wolfpacks preyed on cattle herds much more frequently, especially during the winter months.

Wolfing was common among cowboys in this period, for stockmen and government agencies offered a bounty on the hides of predatory wolves. In 1884, the first year that a one-dollar bounty was offered for a dead wolf in Montana, 5,450 carcasses were recorded; by 1918, when the wolf bounty programs were halted in the state, 80,730 wolves had been exterminated.

The most common method of killing these animals was to lace meat with strychnine, and it is quite possible that the cowboys in Russell's watercolor intend to use the antelope carcass for bait. Unfortunately, that practice could kill much more than the wolves. The Indians greatly disapproved of it, for they lost horses, livestock, and even some of their own number to the indiscriminate use of poison on the range.

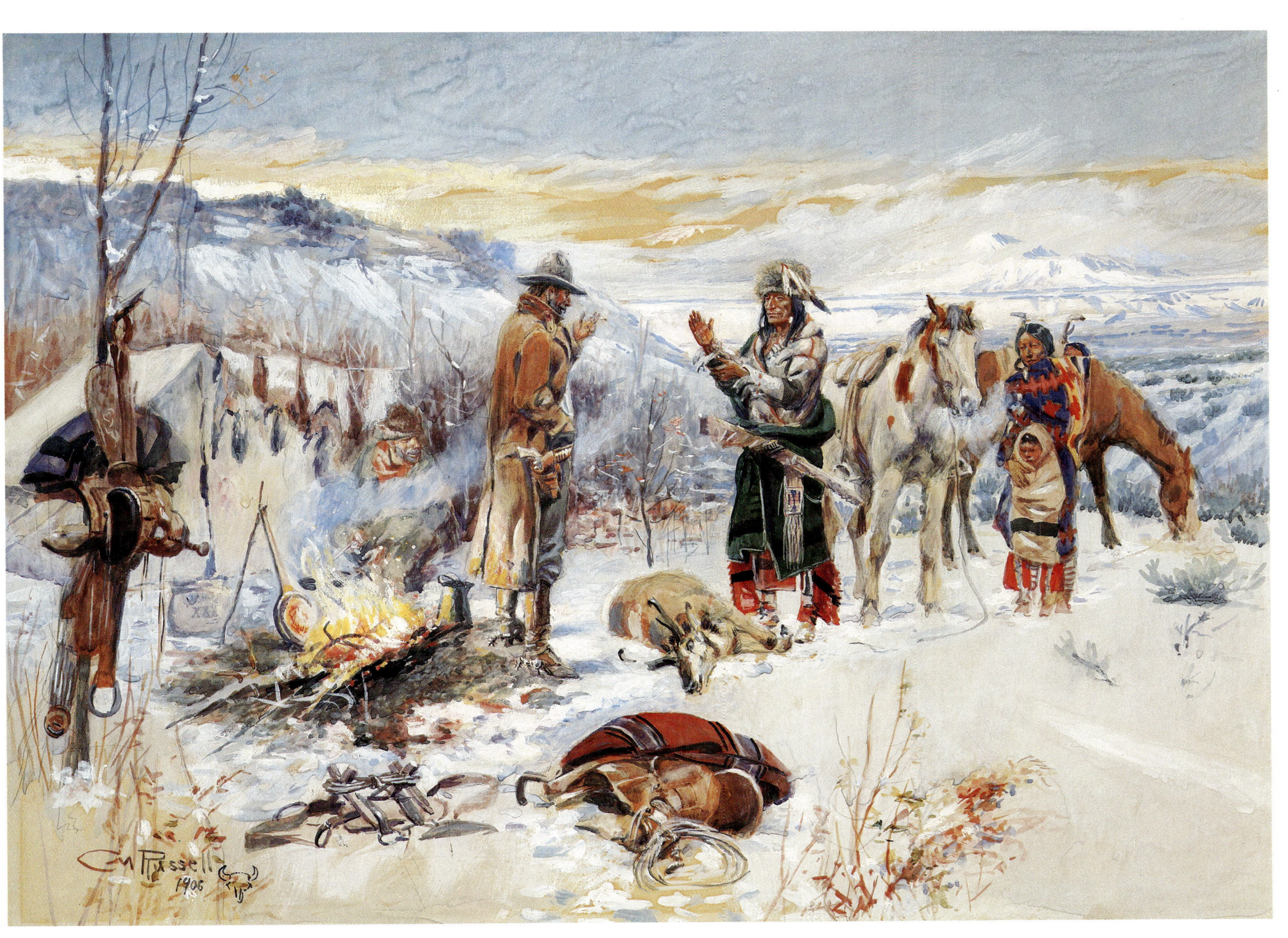

The Medicine Man

1908, oil on canvas, 30 x 48⅛ inches

Soon after this painting was completed, Russell's contemporaries hailed it as one of his finest works. The artist himself described the subject on April 24, 1911, in a letter to Willis Sharpe Kilmer, who purchased the painting out of an exhibition of Russell's work at the Folsom Galleries in New York. "'The Medicine Man' I consider one of the best pieces of my work and these few words may give you some idea of the meaning of the picture," Russell wrote.

The medicine man among the Plains Indians often had more to do with the movements of his people than the chief and he is supposed to have the power to speak with the spirits and the animals. This painting represents a band of Blackfeet Indians with their Medicine Man in the foreground. The landscape was taken from a sketch I made on Loan [sic] Tree Creek in the Judith Basin and I remember when this was

game country. The mountain range in the background is the Highwood with Haystack and Steamboat Buttes to the right. The Blackfeet once claimed all country from Saskatchewan south to the Yellowstone and one of their favorite hunting grounds was the Judith Basin. This country today is fenced and settled by ranchmen and farmers with nothing but a few deep worn trails where once walked the buffalo but I am glad Mr. Kilmer I knew it before nature's enemy the white man invaded and marred its beauty.

In Russell's painting, the striking figure of the Medicine Man, astride his pinto horse, leads the way. He sits erect in his saddle, gazing proudly ahead while the other warriors and the rest of the village string out to either side behind him. The medicine man wears an antelope-horn medicine pendant around his neck, and white ermine skins dangle from the feather medallion on the side of his head. His

face and body are painted with designs in red, the most obtainable earth color that the Blackfeet employed. A decorated buffalo robe is slung across his saddle, and on his back he wears a painted shield, made from the thick hide of a buffalo bull's neck and treated in a firepit to make it even tougher. The warrior riding on the left is wearing a hooded coat made from a Hudson's Bay blanket, like traditional ones worn by the early French Canadian trappers.

The medicine man holds a crooked lance trimmed with a scalplock and feathers in his right hand. Russell maintained to Joe DeYong, one of his protégés, that "where the head man stuck his lance in the ground is where the women put up their lodges. These men were called wolf men by the Blackfeet. If a Blackfoot said a man was a wolf it was no insult it meant the man was very smart. In the sign language wolf and smart are the same."

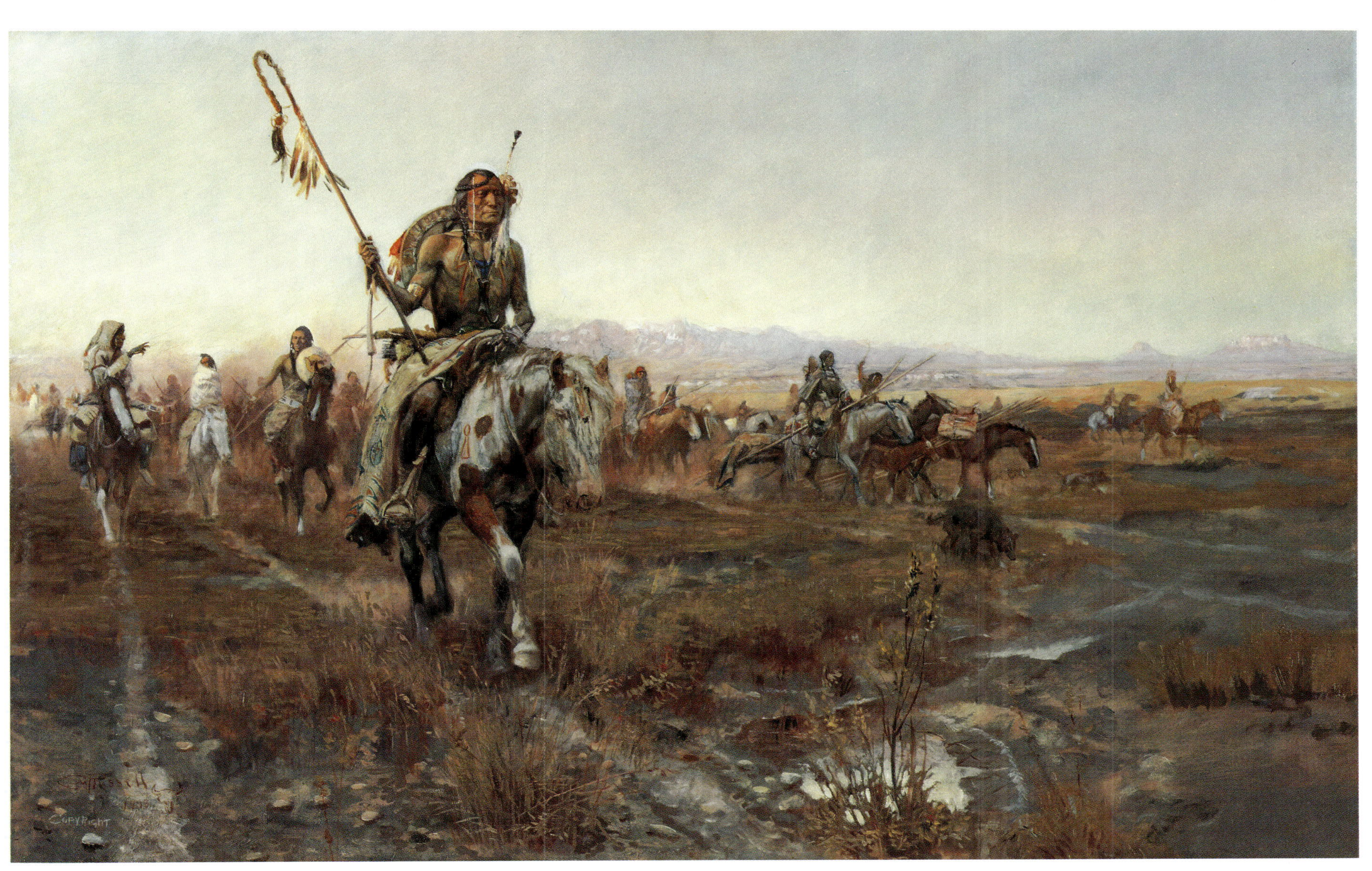

Smoke of a .45

1908, oil on canvas, 24⅜ x 36¼ inches

Gambling was widespread in frontier towns, and some of the most persistent participants were cowboys. Livestock owners struggled to prevent gambling in the camps or on cattle trails, but there was little they could do when the cowpunchers headed into town on their free time. Although many people railed against gambling as a vice, most frontier townsfolk looked the other way since there was profit involved. Indeed, a professional gambler was often viewed as a positive economic force, especially by the owner of a saloon. Not surprisingly, the gamblers usually won, and given human nature, a cowboy often played until he had lost all his wages.

This painting, a spirited rendition of a fracas between a group of cowboys and the inhabitants of a gambling saloon on the Montana frontier in the 1880s, attracted much attention when it was exhibited in Chicago and New York in 1911. In the latter city, Russell was hailed as "the painter of the West that has passed," and his life as well as his art began evolving into legend and myth. "For years he was a trailer of cattle, a hunter among the Indians, a bronco buster, a husky, vigorous dweller in the open, and the things of those days are a part of him now," one worshipful writer exaggerated. "His hand is still quick at his pistol, and dextrous in throwing the lariat."

Of course, such a reputation did nothing to hurt the sale of Russell's art, and subjects like *Smoke of a .45* were very popular. The painting was originally created for the Ridgley Calendar Company, who exhibited it in their window in Great Falls in February 1908 before shipping it out for reproduction. "A bunch of cowpunchers have been playing poker in the saloon, and the game has ended in a rough house, which terminated in a free-for-all fight, the saloon men and gamblers on one side and the cowpunchers on the other," a writer noted in the *Great Falls Daily Tribune*.

Russell's unexcelled ability as an artist and storyteller is readily apparent in this work. The composition of interwoven men and horses sweeps the eye from right to left and back again as the action reaches its crescendo. Blue smoke from the gunfire lingers in the air between the figures; the frantic horses lurch in opposite directions, but also in perfect visual counterpoint. Russell manages to compress a great amount of detail into a seamless story line. On the right side of the painting, a string of playing cards lies strewn across the ground beneath the fallen figures, giving mute testimony to the wages of sin.

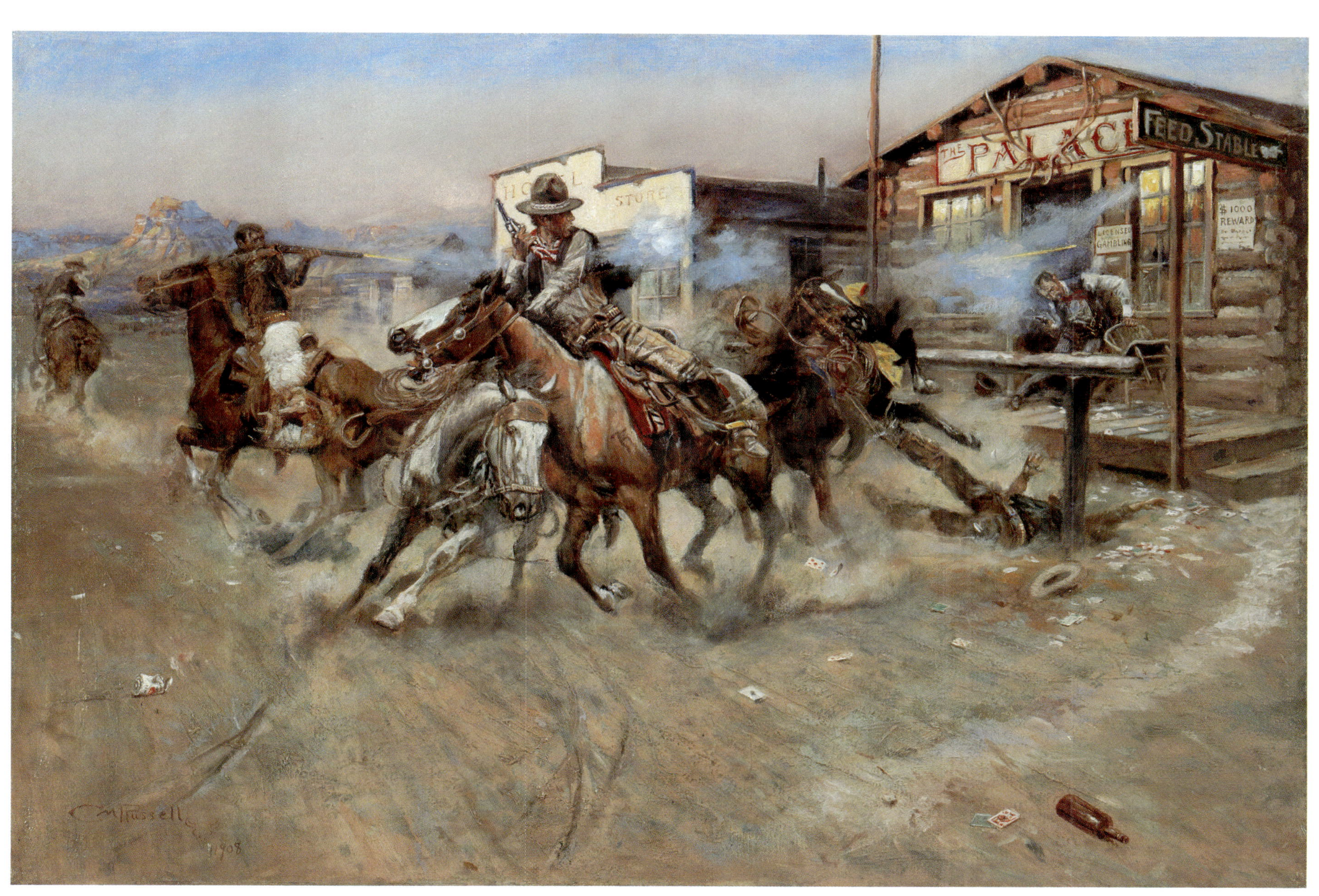

THE PALACE
FEED STABLE
LICENSED GAMBLING
$1000 REWARD
HOTEL
STORE

In Without Knocking

1909, oil on canvas, 20⅛ x 29⅞ inches

Many of Russell's paintings featured real people and events, much to the amusement of his contemporaries. According to local legend, the cowboys in this scene were the artist's fellow riders in the Judith Basin, who decided to enliven the atmosphere around Stanford, Montana, by riding their horses back into the Hoffman saloon, where they had been drinking. Many years later, Hoffman's son recalled the story made famous in Russell's depiction, and he identified some of the riders.

Incidents like this were relatively common in the 1880s and were duly noted in the local newspapers as evidence of minor mischief. On some occasions, the local sheriff would pay a visit to the roundup camp the following day and summon the perpetrators to court, where fines were exacted for damages. These stories, repeated years afterward by Russell and his friends, seemed to get better with every retelling. *In Without Knocking* was among the works Russell exhibited at the Calgary Stampede in 1912; there it was sold to Sir Henry Mill Pellat, one of the wealthiest residents of Toronto. Visiting Englishmen widely praised Russell's works at this exhibition, and within two years the "Cowboy Artist" from Montana was given his first one-man show in London.

As in all his depictions of cowboy life, Russell includes a wealth of fascinating detail. The cowboys' dress and saddle outfits are all somewhat different, reflecting a wide range of influences. The rider second from the left wears a Montana short-brim peak hat, and his pants are typically cuffed, since they were sold as "one size fits all." His finely tooled saddle seems to have a cantle covered with a rattlesnake skin—a talisman originating in Texas and Mexico to ward off saddle sores. The horses are wonderfully rendered, particularly the one that has just thrust its foreleg through the floorboards on the porch. The rider adroitly steps off his fallen mount while the others ride past him. Playing cards, blue poker chips, and a lone beer bottle litter the ground, adding to the sense of disorder and confusion, while the holes on the sign above the cowboys' heads indicate that it has been used as a target more than once in the past.

"That painting has become a classic," one writer noted more than forty years later. "I remember one Tom Mix epic in which the director ordered a re-take of a saloon raiding scene, just in order to have a horse plunge a foot through the board sidewalk. He had seen that in Charlie Russell's painting."

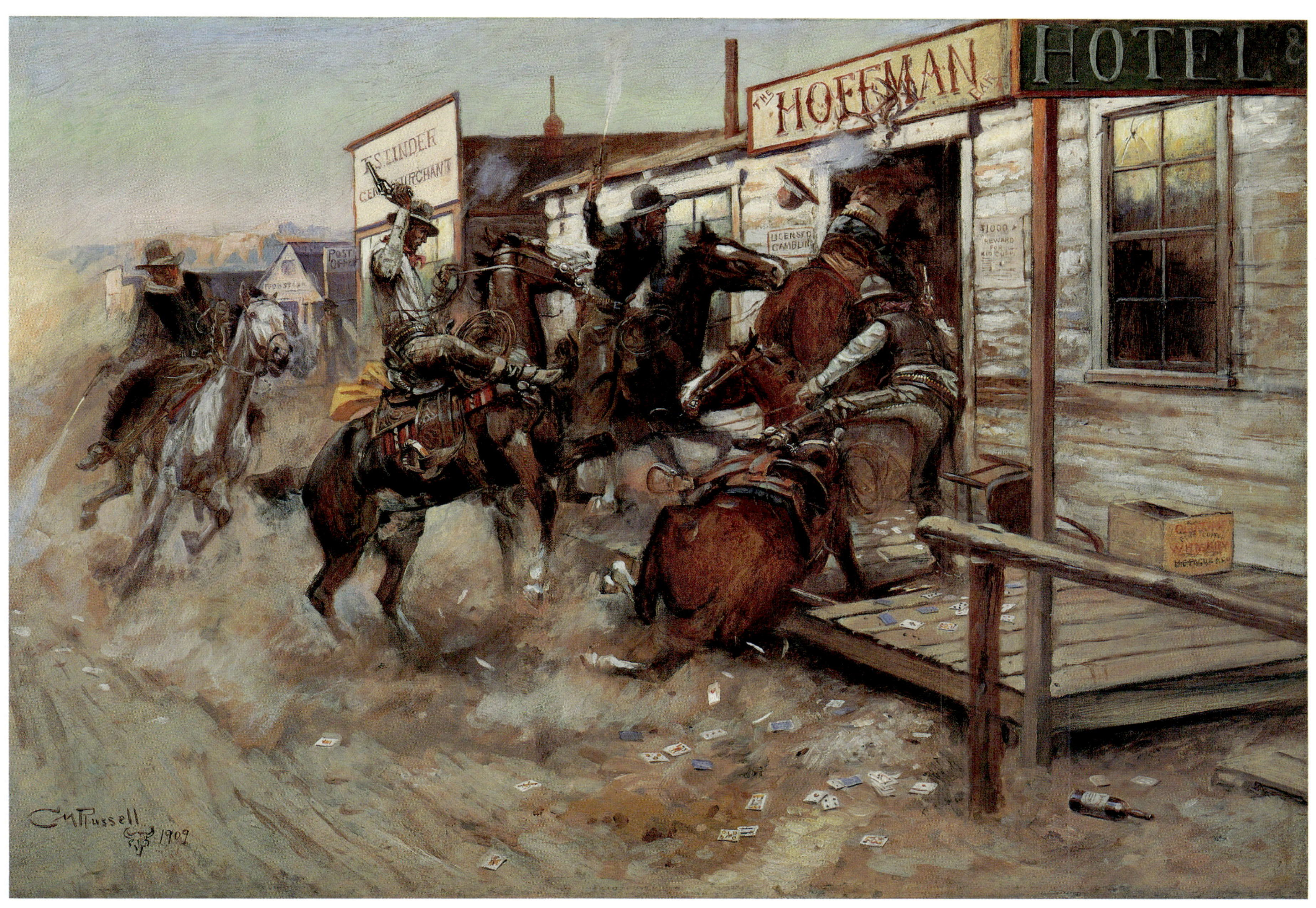
T.S. LINDER
GEN'L MERCHANT
POST OFFICE
THE HOFFMAN BAR
HOTEL &
LICENSED GAMBLING
$1000 REWARD
C M Russell 1909

When Horseflesh Comes High

1909, oil on canvas, 24⅛ x 36⅛ inches

Stock rustling was a major problem on the Montana cattle ranges in the early 1880s, when grazing areas were still large. Embattled livestock owners often were forced to take matters into their own hands. Granville Stuart, a pioneer ranchman whose nephew Bob was a good friend of Russell's, wrote in 1883: "Near our home ranch we discovered one rancher whose cows invariably had twin calves and frequently triplets, while the range cows in that vicinity were all barren and would persist in hanging around this man's corral, envying his cows their numerous children and bawling and lamenting their own childless fate. This state of affairs continued until we were obliged to call around that way and threaten to hang the man if his cows had any more twins." Following the spring roundup in 1884, a group met at Stuart's ranch to form a vigilante organization that would counteract the outbreak of rustling. Within a few months they tracked down and captured or hanged a number of suspects and, near the mouth of the Musselshell River, fought a gun battle with an organized gang, killing the leader and most of his followers.

The *Cheyenne Democratic Leader* of August 10, 1884, reported another incident on the Musselshell. A group of cowboys staked out a suspicious log cabin, where "several small parties came and went; some by day and others by night, having in their possession horses evidently stolen." Realizing it was a rustler's den, the cowboys attacked it, killed a number of the inhabitants, and burned it to the ground. "There never was a period in the history of this or any other Territory when so much horse thieving was going on," the newspaper concluded. "The citizens are determined to effectually stop it. Fully thirty thieves have been hanged or shot in the past month." Most of this kind of vigilante activity ended by April 1885, when the Montana Stockgrowers Association was formed in part to counteract lawlessness on the open range.

Russell's painting once again immortalizes a scene from the early days of the open range. The canvas, exhibited at the 1912 Calgary Stampede and purchased by Sir Henry Pellat, shows a group of horse rustlers who have been overtaken by a sheriff's posse or ranchmen. One shot has downed a rustler's horse, and the outlaw desperately returns fire from the ground. His partner, dressed in a "half-breed" costume that includes a bright red sash around the waist, makes haste to mount his horse for a fast getaway. Russell has heightened the sense of drama by placing the viewer among the horse thieves, as part of the immediate danger.

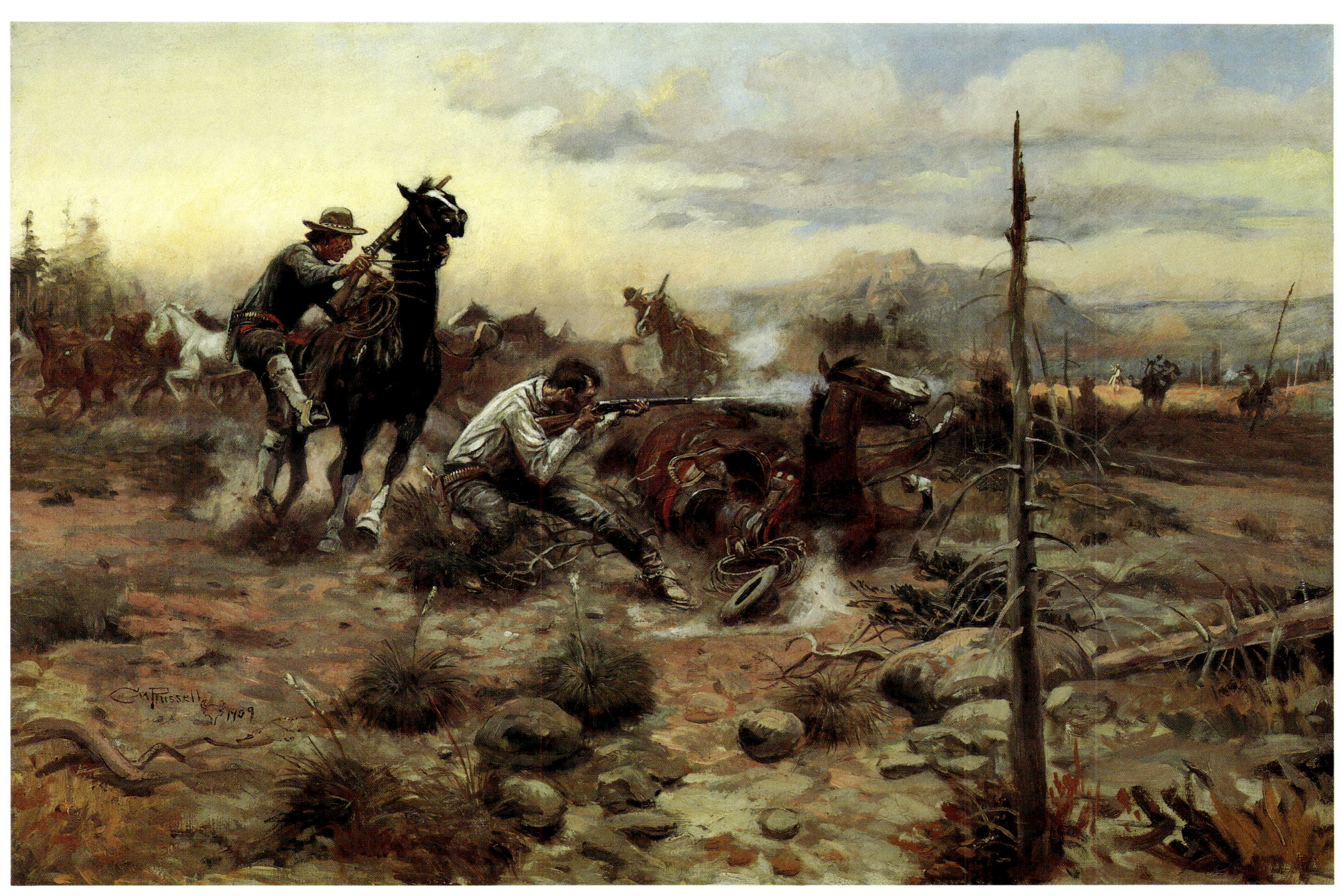

Wild Horse Hunters

1913, oil on canvas, 30 x 46⅞ inches

In *The Mustangs* (1952), J. Frank Dobie observed that: "Halted in animated expectancy or running in abandoned freedom, the mustang was the most beautiful, the most spirited and the most inspiriting creature ever to print foot on the grasses of America." These animals—whose name was an English corruption of the Spanish *mesteña*, meaning wild horse stock—were legendary for their acuity of sight and smell, especially when man was present. By Russell's time, small bands of mustangs, each dominated by a stallion, roamed throughout the West.

Of this painting, with its group of cowboys, or mustangers, at work, Nancy Russell wrote: "The wild horse is the wildest of all animals. . . .In a level country it is almost impossible for any rider, no matter how good his mount, to get near enough to use a rope. These riders have cut-banked a bunch by running them into a pocket in the Badlands where they have them cornered."

As the riders come from opposite ends of a gully, the frightened mustangs attempt to scramble up its steep sides. One cowboy, having roped the black stallion that leads the band, has taken his dallies and deftly swings his weight away from the saddle to assist his struggling horse. The other riders move in to aid the successful roper, who by all accounts should have a real fight on his hands. The danger to both horse and horseman is clear in Dobie's story of a Texas cowboy who cornered a mustang band in a ravine and managed to rope the stallion; the cowboy expected the horse to "run to the end of the rope, but before he tightened it he headed straight for me, ready to grab. He came pawing and caught my right thigh down towards the knee between his teeth." In the melee, the stallion was killed and the wounded cowboy was lucky to escape with his life.

One of the more striking aspects of *Wild Horse Hunters* is Russell's use of vibrant color. Vivid tones of blue, pink, and lavender flow across the background and melt into the shadows of the ravine, contrasting with the strong earth colors of the rocks and undergrowth. "His colors have been criticized for their flashiness," one critic noted in the *Chicago Herald* when Russell exhibited a number of his paintings in that city in February 1911. "It is true that certain of his skies forming the background for the spirited action of the foreground savor of the tinted picture postal card, but Mr. Russell defends this arrangement warmly, claiming that it is true to life and that every ranchman and Indian who ever saw his pictures was satisfied with the coloring." Russell could claim that such color effects were realistic, but he also was well aware that the work of artists like Maxfield Parrish, whose use of vivid colors sometimes bordered on garish, was very much in vogue.

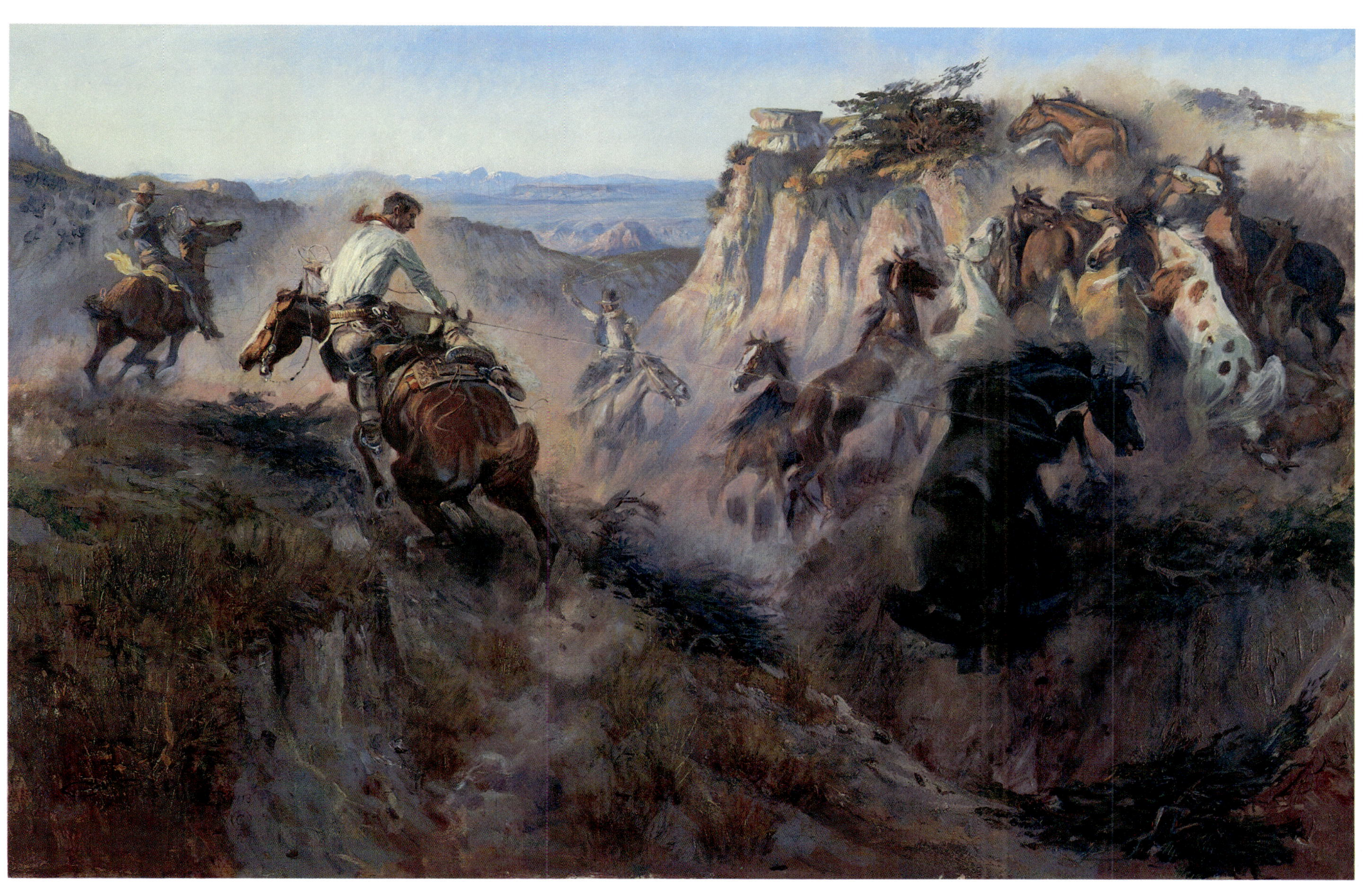

Antelope and *Bighorn Ram*

Left: 1915, wax, plaster, paint, and hemp, 7⅝ x 6¾ x 4⅝ inches
Right: 1915, wax, plaster, paint, and hemp, 7¼ x 6¼ x 5¼ inches

While Russell was well known to his contemporaries as a painter, his reputation as a modeler was legendary. Indeed, Russell himself often told people that he thought his abilities as a sculptor were superior to his skills with paint, and few disagreed with him. "He could do the most amazing things without looking at them," one lady recalled about Russell's early days in the Judith Basin. "A lump of clay worked under the table would appear as a horse, or a bear, or perhaps an Indian. He found a deposit of very smooth terra cotta clay in the river bank. This provided material for figures and groups that could be found in many cabins up and down the valley." Later, when Russell was more estabished as an artist, he carried lumps of beeswax in his pockets and modeled them as he talked or listened. Many remarked on the artist's long, slender fingers; photographs reveal that some of his nails were long and pointed, doubtless to serve as built-in modeling tools.

The sister of John Marchand, a noted illustrator and friend of Russell's who sponsored the artist's early visits to New York, remembered how Russell would tell his stories while "his hands were busy working with bits of wax which he carried in his pockets. From time to time he placed on the window sill a little wax pig —or a dog or a tired hungry wolf—each little figure full of individuality and character."

Russell was a consummate artist of wildlife subjects, and it is likely that he learned much of his natural history under the tutelage of Jake Hoover, the skilled hunter and trapper whom the artist accompanied during his first two years in Montana. Joe DeYong, who was one of the few people to receive art instruction from Russell, maintained that the older artist had a "primitive" understanding of wild animals and an ability to instill a mixture of wariness, alertness, fear, craftiness, appetite—in short, instinct—in all his subjects.

The four models illustrated here demonstrate Russell's three-dimensional skills. The animals are frozen at a point of action that seems wholly naturalistic, with every muscle and sinew carefully detailed. Russell usually modeled his figures first, before stiffening them with wire, because he felt he could capture the natural movement of the subject most effectively without the confines of an armature. The base, cast separately in plaster, always came later. He usually sealed both wax and plaster with a hot mixture of linseed oil and powdered rosin before applying any color. For the tufts of grass, he often used shredded pieces of hemp because it was durable.

In addition to creating finished pieces like these, Russell often worked out problems of light and shadow in his paintings by first modeling figures or groups—a technique he urged all of his illustrator friends, including Marchand, to follow.

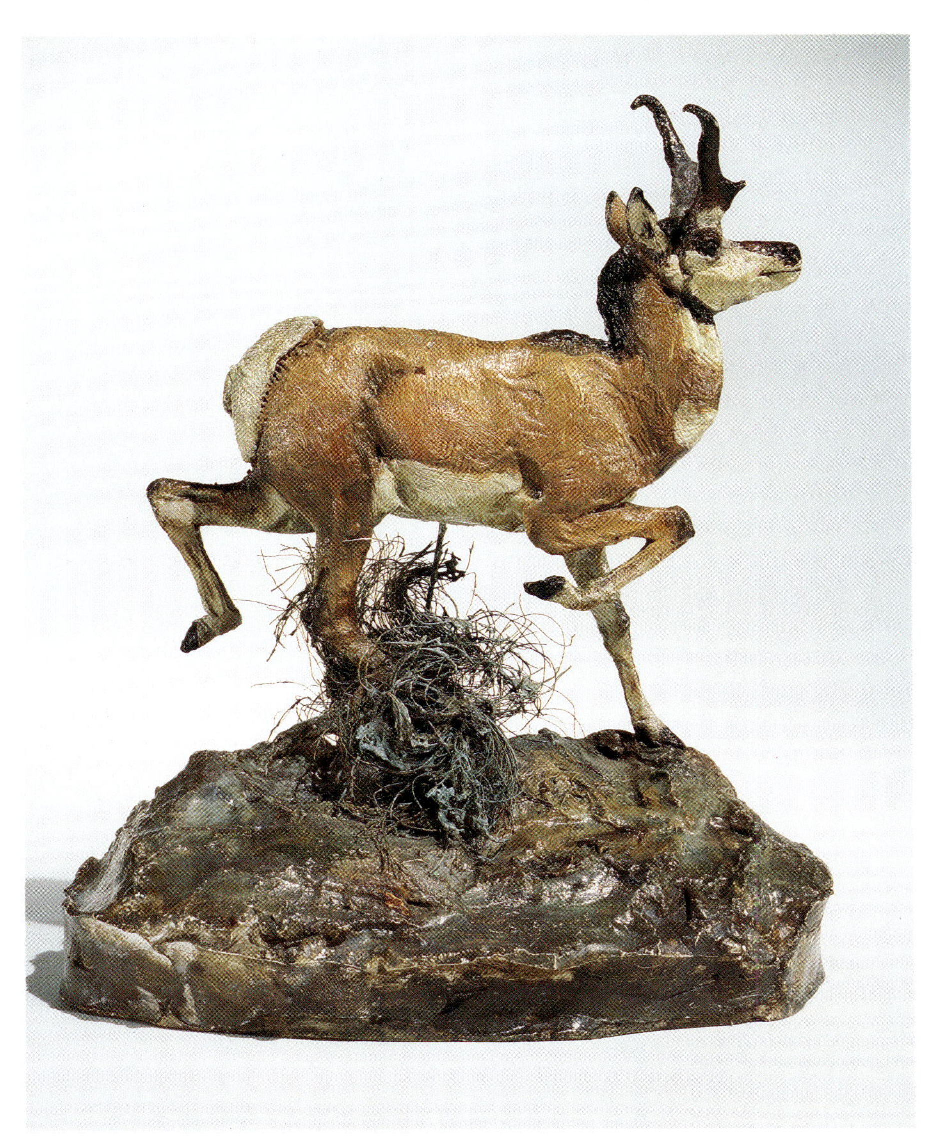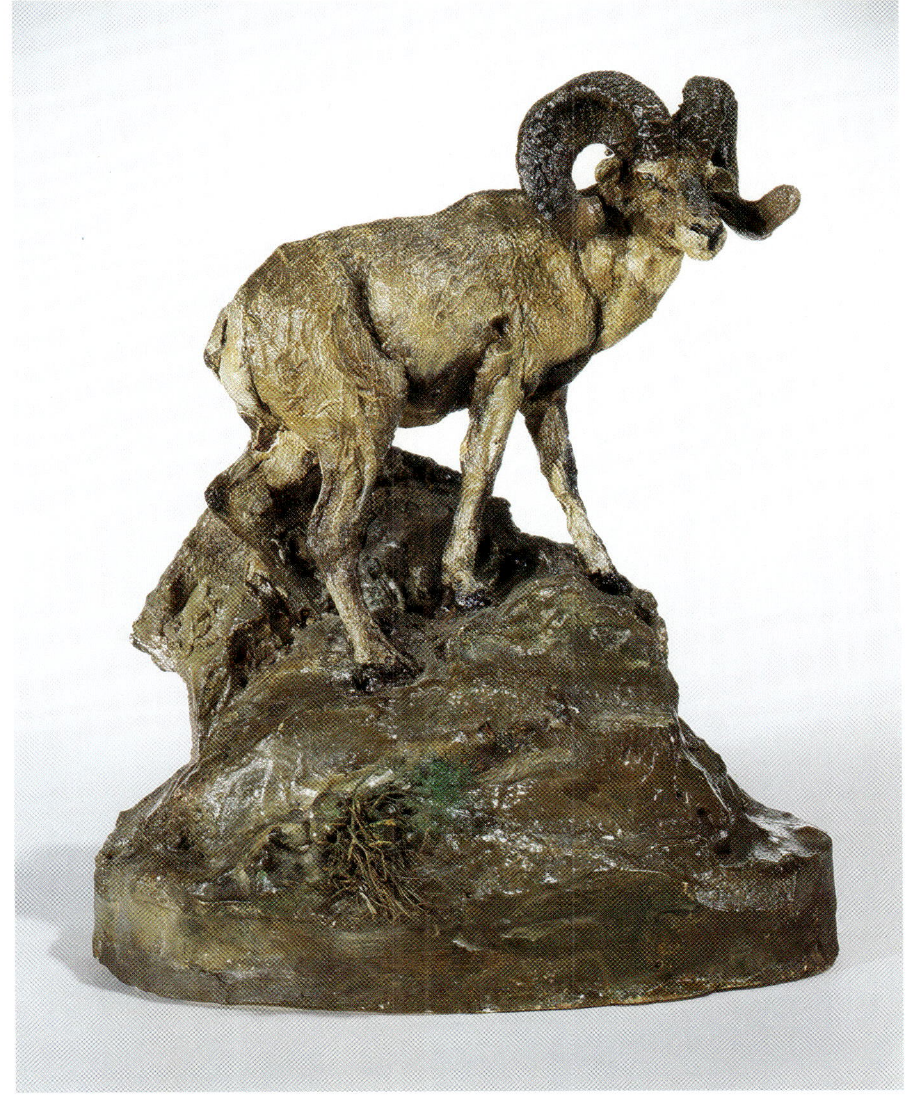

Grizzly

1915, wax, plaster, paint, and hemp, 5⅜ x 8 x 4⅞ inches

Wolf

1915, wax, plaster, paint, and hemp, 5¼ x 7⅞ x 4¼ inches

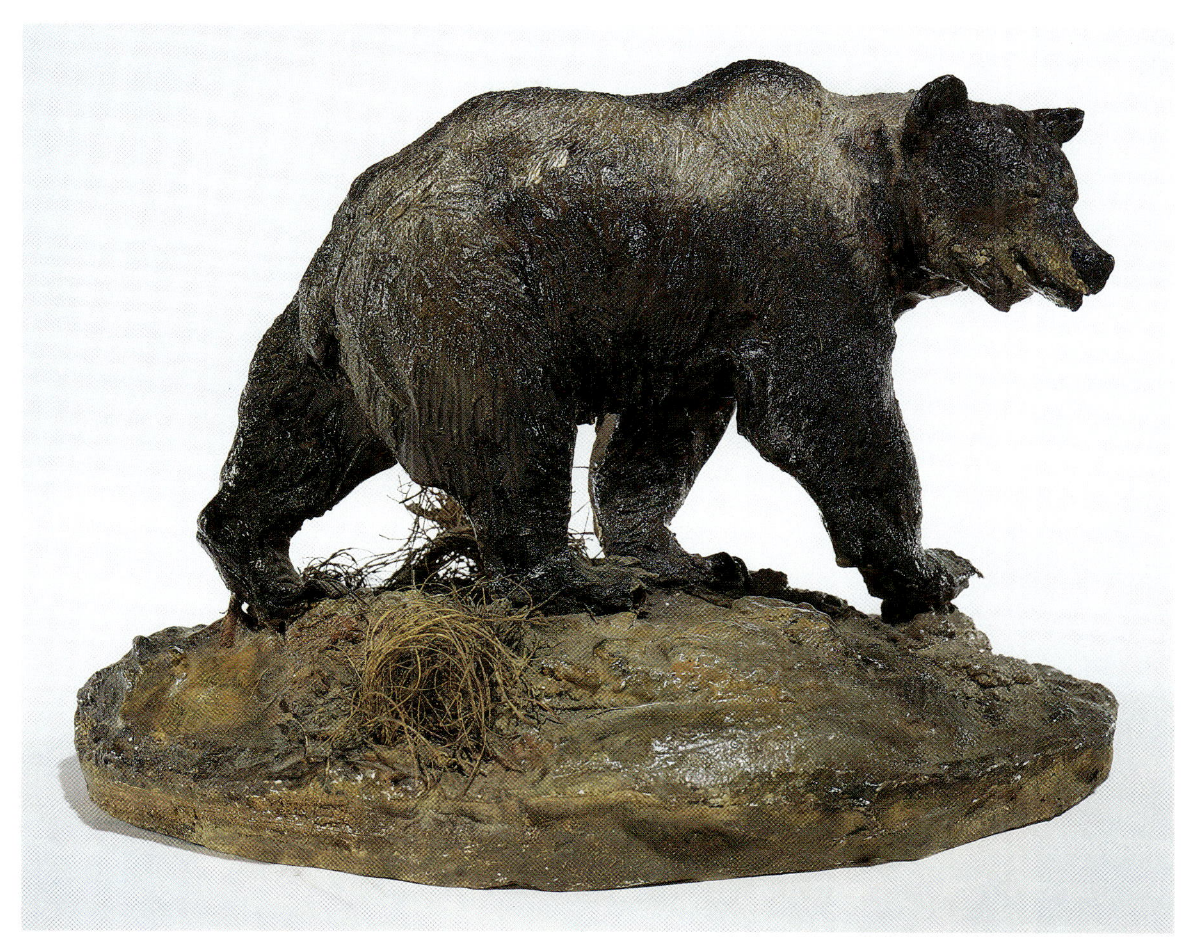

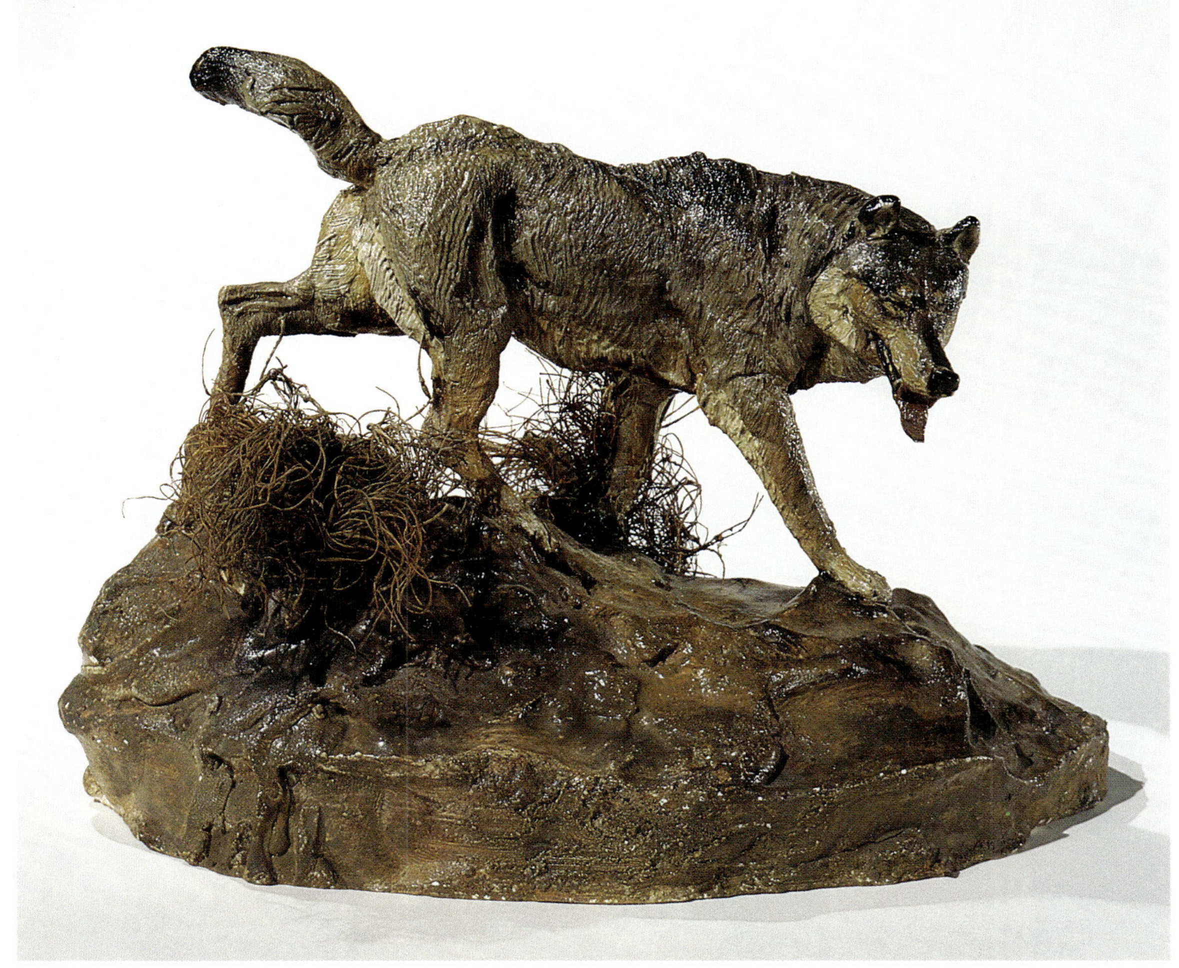

The Price of His Hide

1915, oil on canvas, 24 x 36 inches

This dramatic rendition of hunters violently encountering a grizzly bear at close quarters is reminiscent of the stories told by Russell's contemporary, William H. Wright. A hunter-naturalist who made a lifelong study of grizzlies, Wright had gained his knowledge from his career as a hunter. "The best way to hunt them," he wrote, "is to study their habits, familiarize yourself with their range, and lie in wait for them near their feeding grounds." His book *The Grizzly Bear*, published in 1909 and still one of the most interesting accounts ever written on the subject, uses many of Wright's own experiences to detail how difficult the bears are to track. "Not only is the grizzly phenomenally quick to catch every sound, not only is his sense of smell amazingly developed, but he is particularly cunning in guarding himself against danger from the rear, and his senses are at least matched by his shrewdness."

Wright viewed the grizzly bear as central to the history of the American West, beginning with its first sighting by Lewis and Clark in 1805. A little more than a century later, however, the great beast, named *Ursus horribilis* by early naturalists, seemed on its way to extinction. As the frontier became more settled and the number of bears dwindled, Wright found himself tracking grizzlies not to hunt them, but to study them.

Russell always called himself "a harmless hunter." Throughout his life he accompanied friends on extended hunting and fishing trips, but he never desired to hunt. Instead, he enjoyed the opportunity to be outdoors, where he could observe the wild animals he had come to know so well during his youthful days in the Little Belt Mountains with Jake Hoover. *The Price of His Hide* is an example of Russell's storytelling at its best: a hunter has narrowly escaped death from the great claws of a charging grizzly, and, as always, the artist has chosen the perfect moment to stop the action of the story and present it to the viewer. The hapless hunter's Winchester lies at the lower right, apparently lost early in the struggle. The wounded man's exhaustion and relief contrast sharply with the exhilaration of his comrade, who lifts his hat in triumph as the bear's great bulk hangs across a fallen log, its massive claws stilled. Surely no artist painted the grizzly bear, even in death, with more authority than Russell.

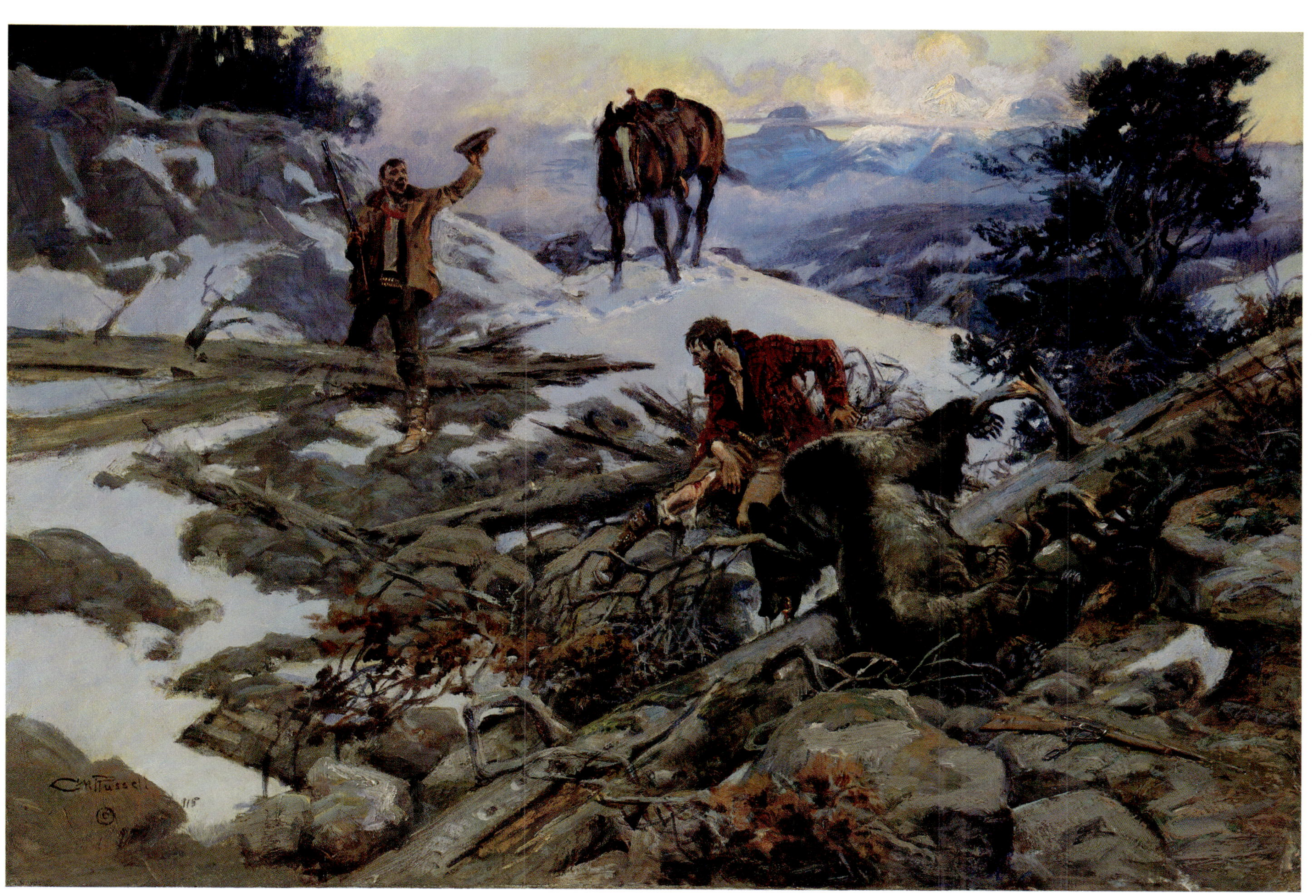

Loops and Swift Horses Are Surer than Lead

1916, oil on canvas, 30⅛ x 48⅛ inches

The incident depicted in this painting actually took place in 1904, in the Milk River country of northeastern Montana. The story was often related in roundup camps and bunkhouses, and the several versions recorded for posterity differ only in minor details. Wallace Coburn, a close friend of Russell's who was working on the spring roundup that day, supposedly related the story to the artist. On the morning of June 1, a night herder returned with his remuda to roundup camp in the Larb Hills, near the head of Larb and Timber Creeks. He was missing about forty saddle horses from the string, and according to Walt Coburn—Wallace's half-brother and a writer of western fiction—that cowboy "was the butt of a lot of rough joshing and hoorawing because of the horses he had spilled." The embattled nighthawk insisted that something had persistently stampeded the horses, but this only increased the derision heaped upon him. The wagon boss of the roundup, Bill Jaycox, detailed several cowpunchers to look for the missing mounts, then led the rest of his men on morning circle to scatter and work the rough country. About three or four miles from camp, Jaycox spotted the missing horses, bunched and running toward the camp as if they were frightened by something, just as the nighthawk had claimed. At that moment, three cowboys—Joe Reynolds, Frank Howe, and Charlie Shufeldt—encountered the horses at much closer range and realized they were being chased by a large bear.

The three cowhands unlooped their lariats and headed straight for the bear, which reared up on its hind legs to confront them. The first cowboy to throw his rope was young Charlie, known as the "Shufeldt Kid" to his peers. "The loop missed its throw by a narrow margin," Coburn related, "and the spooked bronc bogged its head and commenced pitching and snorting." The Shufeldt Kid is shown struggling with his horse at the left of Russell's painting. The other two cowboys also missed, but as the bear attempted a getaway, Reynolds managed to rope one of its legs, flipping it up, as shown to the right. Howe then head-roped the bear, both riders dally-wrapped their ropes and stood the horses off, and the snarling animal lay stretched upon the ground as additional cowboys rushed up to assist. Contrary to what Russell has shown, "nary a cowpuncher there packed a six-shooter that morning." They had to dispatch the bear with rocks and knives, giving Wallace Coburn the skin as a trophy to hang at his ranch. Russell also claimed an artist's prerogative with another detail: all the participants stated the animal was a big female cinnamon bear, not the more ferocious silvertip grizzly shown here.

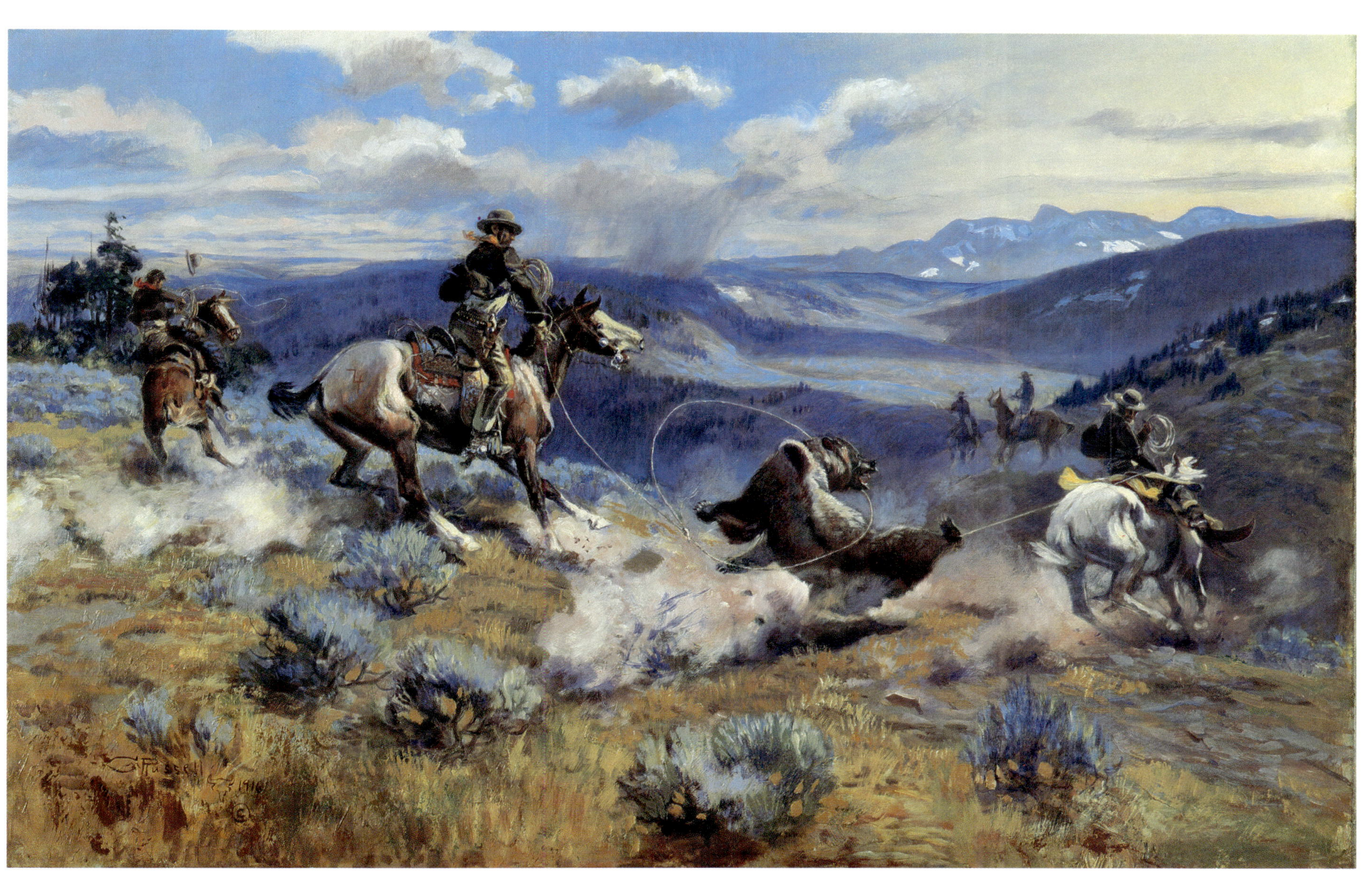

The Buffalo Hunt No. 39

1919, oil on canvas, 30⅛ x 48⅛ inches

According to several sources, Russell considered this painting to be the best version of the Indian buffalo hunt that he ever painted, and Nancy Russell herself pronounced it "one of the finest things Charlie ever did." The artist apparently selected the painting for the collection of his lifelong friend, Will Rogers, and it remained the humorist's favorite until his untimely death. In 1948 Amon Carter acquired the work from Rogers' family.

As in his earlier versions of the subject, Russell concentrated on the moment when the mounted Indian hunters overtake a stampeding band of buffaloes from opposite directions, forcing the animals to tumble over each other in panic and allowing the warriors to close in and pick off the cows or calves. Russell arranged the figures in a tight composition that occupies center stage in the broad Sun River landscape, with the blue-shouldered outline of Square Butte in the right background. A Blackfoot warrior, his face and arms decorated with red paint, loosens his arrows into a slathering buffalo cow that has just trampled her calf. The Indian's white horse is brightly decorated, its beautifully rendered skin reflecting every color of Russell's palette. A feather has been tied into its tail as a talisman, and the red handprint on its neck is a sign that the warrior has ridden over an enemy in battle.

Beginning in 1908, Russell participated in a much-publicized annual roundup of buffalo that were being sent from the Flathead Indian reservation to Canada to form the nucleus of a new national herd. Two years later, he was able to observe the animals at close range when he became one of the herders assigned to control the running buffalo. That turned out to be "no small job," according to the artist. On one occasion, he and his fellow riders encountered a bull "about the size of a murphy wagon with tassels all over him and black tongue hanging out [which] made us excuse ourselves." The bull narrowly missed Russell, who confessed, "I tell you, for a second or two my hair didn't lay good." Despite this, the artist gained invaluable knowledge about the animals, and he subsequently employed it in the work illustrated here. According to one of his friends, "he found the bulls would hurdle out of a tightly compressed herd and so put two animals doing this in the painting." But Russell didn't stop there: "He got the Blackfeet Indians to criticize it and made some changes and when completed he said he had put on canvas a true painting of an historic past action of Indians killing buffalo with bows and arrows."

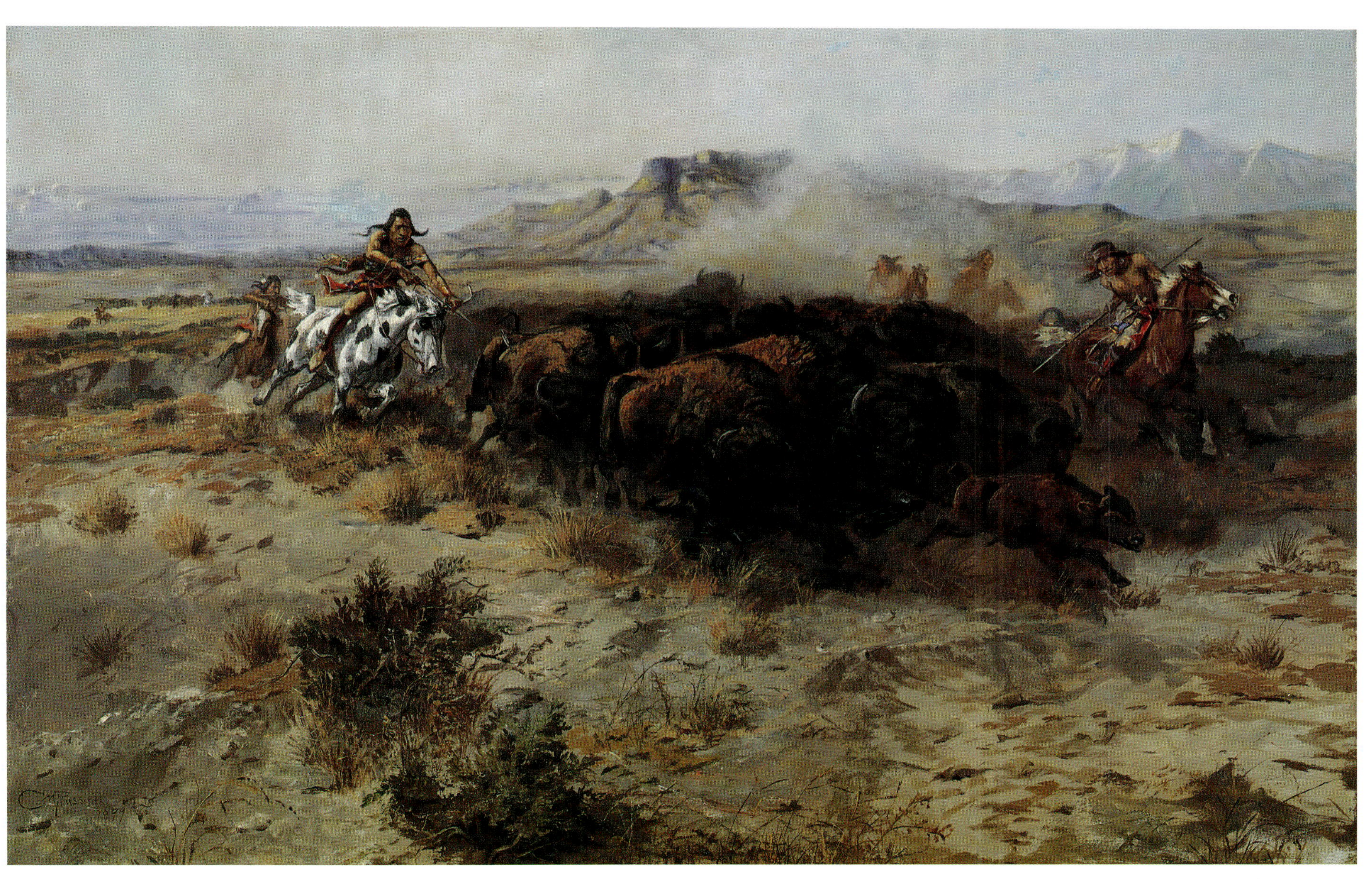

A *Tight Dally and a Loose Latigo*

1920, oil on canvas, 30¼ x 48¼ inches

When a rider throws a lariat and winds the other end around the saddlehorn several times, it is called "taking a dally." The give in a dallied rope eliminates a sudden stop and is easier on the horse and cow. The latigo is a leather strap fastened at one end to the rigging ring and at the other to the cinch ring, holding the cinch tight under the horse. As the title of this work indicates, problems with a dally or a latigo could put a cowboy into quite a predicament.

Nancy Russell, who owned this painting for many years, left a description of its subject. She pointed out that the cowboy's horse is newly broken—hence the rope hackamore instead of a bridle on his head. A big yearling has run into the taut rope, forcing the horse into a side pull and turning the saddle over. "The stirrups of the turned saddle are hitting this bronc on the hind legs," Nancy Russell wrote, "he is starting to buck and the rider will have to get off or be thrown. All cowpunchers hate to be 'unloaded' so he is staying just as long as possible and has hooked his spur back of the cantle, throwing all of his weight in the left stirrup, trying to get the saddle back in the middle of his horse. If he does not succeed, he will have to get off. Then, the rider that is coming up, swinging his loop, will catch the horse to prevent him from ruining the saddle, which will be hanging under his belly."

Late in his life, Russell wisely observed, "The papers have been kind to me—many times more kind than true. . . . Any man that can make a living doing what he likes is lucky, and I'm that. Any time I cash in now, I win." He died of heart failure on the evening of October 24, 1926, and his funeral in Great Falls attracted tributes from all over the nation. Following his wishes, his body was carried to the cemetery south of town in a horse-drawn funeral wagon, and he was laid to rest in his beloved Montana soil in view of the country he had first known as a youth forty-six years earlier. Soon afterwards Nancy Russell moved into the new home they had been building in Pasadena, California. She named the southwestern-style house Trail's End and filled it with art objects and mementoes of their life together, including this painting. She died on May 24, 1940, and was buried next to her husband.

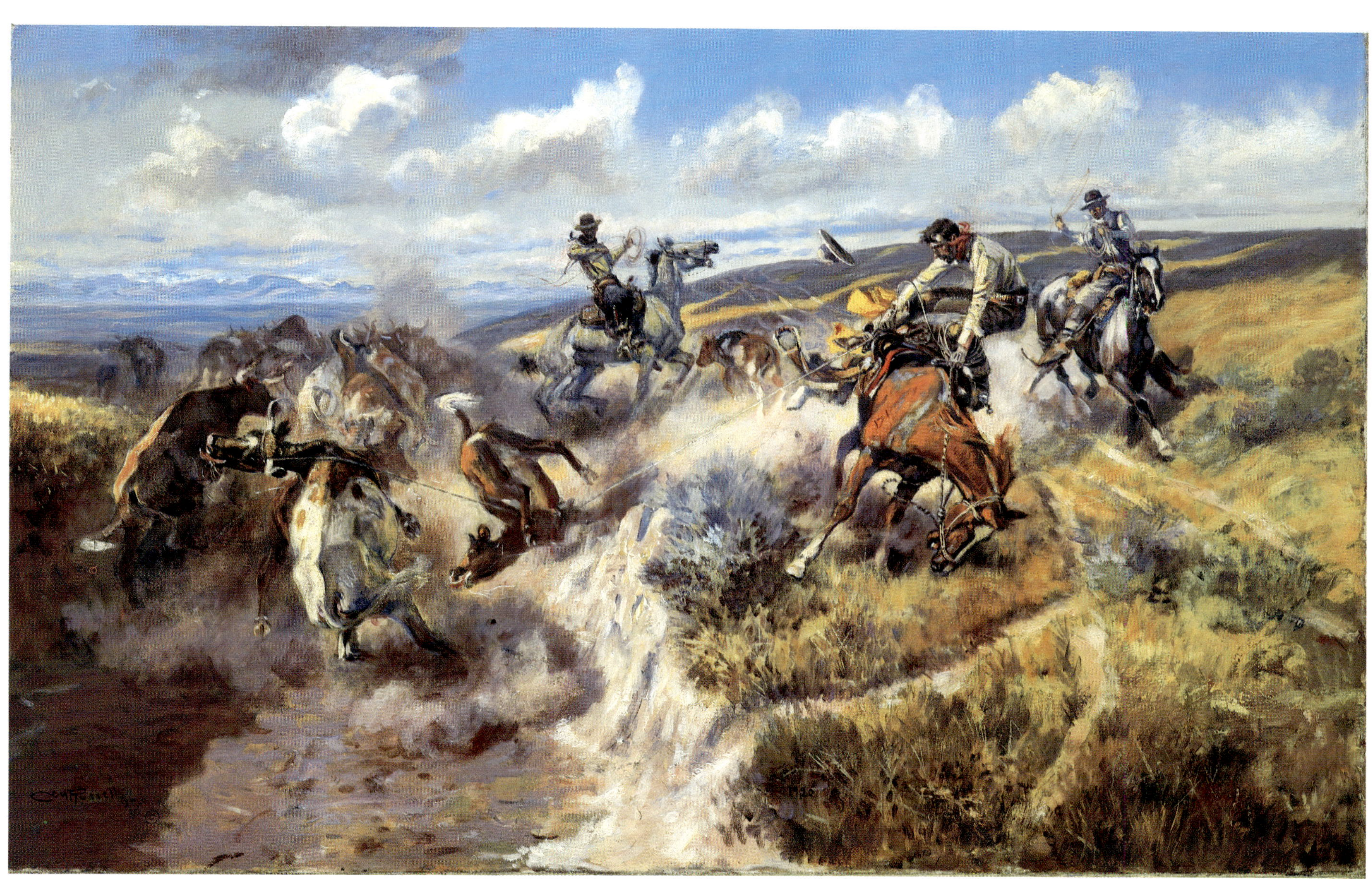

FOR FURTHER READING

Dippie, Brian W. *Looking at Russell*. Fort Worth: Amon Carter Museum, 1987.

——. *Remington and Russell: The Sid Richardson Collection*. Austin: University of Texas Press, 1983.

——. *Word Painter: The Letters of Charles M. Russell*. Fort Worth: Amon Carter Museum, 1993.

Hassrick, Peter. *Charles M. Russell*. New York: Harry N. Abrams in association with the National Museum of American Art, Smithsonian Institution, 1989.

Renner, Frederic G. *Charles M. Russell: Paintings, Drawings and Sculpture in the Amon Carter Museum*. New York: Harry N. Abrams in association with the Amon Carter Museum, 1974.

Renner, Ginger. *A Limitless Sky: The Works of Charles M. Russell*. Flagstaff: Northland Publishing, 1986.

Russell, Austin. *Charles M. Russell, Cowboy Artist*. New York: Twayne Publishers, 1957.

Russell, Charles M. *Good Medicine*. Introductions by Will Rogers and Nancy C. Russell. Garden City, New York: Doubleday, Doran and Company, 1929.

——. *Trails Plowed Under*. Introduction by Will Rogers. New York: Doubleday, Doran and Company, 1927.

Yost, Karl, and Frederic G. Renner. *A Bibliography of the Published Works of Charles M. Russell*. Lincoln: University of Nebraska Press, 1971.